The Radical Party

An Idea for America

DAVID SEBASTIAN ASCHINBERG

ISBN-10: 1483917037

ISBN-13: 9781483917030

Library of Congress Control Number: 2013906504
CreateSpace Independent Publishing Platform
North Charleston, South Carolina

"There's no problem, only solutions."
—John Lennon

Introduction

The difference between how the United States chooses leaders and how dictatorships choose leaders is one choice. We have two choices for President and citizens of dictatorships have one. This is directly due to America's two party system. It is absolutely absurd for the biggest democracy in the world to have only two viable political parties. All over the world countries that are much smaller have several political parties. In fact, the majority of democracies have many more choices, Israel, Italy, France and many others.

My platform is predicated on taking the best ideas regardless of where they come from or who said them in regards to race, gender, religion, or nationality, and using them to create a political party that makes sense and fits my generation, generation X, and the younger ones. By design this book is written so a 13 year old can understand it. I wrote it that way because one of my main messages is that politics needs to be simplified in the U.S. so it is only appropriate that this book is written in a simple manner that is easy to understand. This party is for every rational progressive American. This book will lay down a platform for a third viable political party. The party will be called the Radical Party. My intention is to begin this party as a grass roots movement and build slowly and methodically. We will nominate candidates to run for state legislatures, then congressional posts, and finally to the highest elected positions in the United States. Any outside party that has democratically survived and thrived has followed this recipe for success. As for my own personal ambition, I am an attorney and I plan to run for political office in the not too distant future. By accomplishing these goals I know I can help our country. I will begin by providing a brief account of my life, so you can read my book with the proper perspective of who I am.

I was born in New York City on January 27th, 1974. I have an older brother who was born in New York City on June 23rd, 1972. My father was born in Belgium and raised in Argentina. My mother was born and raised in Argentina. My father is Jewish and my mother is Catholic.

During World War II, when my father was a baby, the Nazis invaded Belgium. Because he was Jewish, if captured, the Nazis would have killed him. To survive my father was hidden and raised by a Catholic family until he was five years old. His father, my grandfather, was arrested by the Gestapo (German secret police) and sent to Auschwitz (a German extermination camp). My grandfather's brothers were murdered there along with one of their wives who was pregnant at the time. After surviving Auschwitz, my grandfather chose to leave all the horrific memories of wartime Europe; he took his family to Argentina to begin a new life. For better or worse, starting when I was three years old, he told me detailed stories of his concentration camp experience.

In the late 1960s military fascist dictatorships were flourishing in Argentina. This means that there were no democratic elections and that military dictators would replace any democratic leadership that was elected. These dictators killed approximately 30,000 of their own people just for having different political views than the dictatorial regime had. These brutal fascist regimes used tactics such as throwing live people from airborne helicopters and placing live rodents inside the vaginas of women. Many former German Nazis, who escaped to Argentina after the war, trained the Argentinian military in these and other torture techniques. Because of these atrocities, that were all too familiar to my father's past experiences with Nazis, my parents believed the United States would be a better place to live and raise a family.

My parents both left Argentina and came to the United States, as young doctors, to finish their medical training. I was raised in an average American way. The only noteworthy difference is that I grew up traveling frequently to South America, to visit relatives, and Western Europe for tourism. My parents wanted me to know what other places in the world were like. From a very young age this gave me an introductory idea of different cultures and people in the world.

I was raised in Joliet, IL, a typical blue-collar mid-western town, where I met the most down-to-earth and genuinely good people that I have ever known. This is an informed opinion because from a very young age I have known several people from all over the country and all over the world. Living in Joliet gave me an excellent idea of what the average American upbringing is. Parents work hard and earn a living, children respect their parents, people take responsibility when they make mistakes and do not pass the buck, and no one treats you better or worse because you are poor or rich, they judge you based on strength of character. I wouldn't trade the environment of my upbringing for anything in the world.

After high school I went to college and I majored in Spanish. Because my parents are from Argentina, I already spoke and wrote Spanish very well, but time was eroding my accent. Majoring in Spanish produced the desired effect of strengthening my accent and introducing me to the world of Spanish literature. After college, I went to law school, graduated and passed the bar exam. After briefly working as an attorney, I began medical school. After some time at medical school I realized that it was not my calling. Politics and writing were my true passions and I wanted to pursue writing this book in earnest. This personal introduction will help put my beliefs in perspective.

I am writing this book to share the core beliefs of a third political party. I take the best ideas of the Republican and Democratic Party and put my spin on them. At the same time I add many of my own ideas. The goal of the Radical Party is to simplify politics while innovating the political landscape as we know it. Ultimately this party is the blue print to making life better for all Americans. I ask that you read this book with an open mind and allow yourself to believe in a radiant future for our country. Most people would rather be the last non-believer than the first believer. It is time to believe that we, unified as a nation, are capable of everything and anything.

Part One

SOCIAL POLICY

The Electoral Process

We are currently facing a crisis where approximately half the population does not vote in Presidential elections. So, effectively, we have Presidents who represent half of the population. When many people wonder why the Presidents never address their concerns, it is because these people do not vote. Most young people, for instance, do not vote. Frankly, apathetic non-voters are not totally to blame for the situation. The system is organized to dissuade potential voters from voting. Specifically, the Electoral College and the primary schedule are to blame. The Electoral College should be abolished immediately.

The Electoral College is a system used for determining the winner of the general election. In this system each state receives a certain number of electoral votes based on their respective populations. For example, California, a big state, gets 55 and New Hampshire, a small state, gets 4. People vote in every state and the candidate who wins gets all of that state's electoral votes. For example, if candidate "A" wins California by one vote he or she would get all 55 of California's electoral votes. This makes no sense and it is not representative of how the people in that state felt. If someone wins California by one vote he or she should be ahead by one vote literally. The outcome of elections should be exclusively based on how the general population votes not on an outdated system. If the only factor in elections was the general population's votes and the Electoral College was thrown out, then every vote would truly count; a vote in a small state would matter just as much as a vote in a large state. The only reason the Electoral College system was put in place originally was because of the colonies.

When the United States first became a country, compromises had to be made to ensure that every colony would join the union. The Electoral College gave more power to big states that were essential to the union, and that were instrumental in forming the country. This is no longer the case; two hundred years plus have passed and we are no longer in danger of losing big states from the union. Therefore, this should no longer be the rationale in forming a logical system to choose our most important leader, especially when the current system dissuades many potential voters from voting.

The current system is one of the reasons people do not vote. They do not think that their vote counts and a lot of the time it does not. For instance, take a Republican in IL, a state that will almost assuredly elect a Democrat, his vote is a waste of time. This Republican's vote will not be represented at all in the Electoral College. However, if we abandon the Electoral College, then this would not be an issue. Using the pure popular vote model, everyone's vote would count and it could make a difference. One vote could theoretically decide the Presidency. Regardless of how you feel about Al Gore or George W. Bush, you must admit that if we had the popular vote system it would have affected the 2000 election. Al Gore had the majority of the popular vote but George W. Bush had more Electoral College votes so he won. I use this example to show you how it can make a difference.

The system for primaries is also flawed. As it stands now, primaries in different states are held on different days, with some states being grouped together. States like Iowa and New Hampshire, two states that are totally non-representative of the racial and religious diversity of our nation, have very early primaries. That is why you hear so much about candidates spending so much time in these states early on in campaigns. Once these early states pick their winners this starts impacting the election as a whole because the media puts a front-runner tag on a candidate and this affects the way others vote. Campaign donors start throwing big money behind the candidate who has the front-runner status and they stop donating to candidates who are polling third and fourth for instance. This forces lesser candidates to end their campaigns prematurely; they run out of money before most of America has had a chance to vote. Theoretically a candidate (the front-runner) could have the election wrapped up after leading the first ten states that vote and before the rest of the forty states have even had their say. The states with the earliest primaries have much more of an impact than the states with the later primaries. There is no reason why New Hampshire's votes should be more important than another state's that decide by the time the election is over. How democratic is that? The solution to this problem is easy.

One way to ensure that everyone's vote does count is to have every primary on the same day. If the U.S. can do it for the general election, it should be done for the primaries as well. If every state voted on the last day of the primary cycle, then candidates would be able to campaign nationally and all of America would be able to get to know all the candidates. Instead of candidates going to 100 diners in Iowa, to really get to know the people, they could go to diners in every state across the country to get to know all Americans. Further, money would not dry up as quickly for lesser candidates and they would have more time to run a national campaign. There is no logical argument against having the primaries all on the same day. These changes would jumpstart the electorate, they would realize that their votes truly count, the entire country would get to know the candidates, it would not be over after the first couple of primaries, and every vote could really make a difference. But all of this would not be enough to get every American to vote.

Because it is so crucial to document what candidate people want to be their President, in addition to the above-mentioned measures, a law should be passed that makes it illegal not to vote. The consequence to not voting could be some minor fine like $100.00. You would be surprised how many people would vote. Many countries have this type of system. For example, Australia fines citizens $500.00 for not voting and it is effective. Obviously people could still write in a candidate or have an option to not vote for any of the candidates. But, it would be documented. Voting should also be easier, for example voting via email or some type of system where people can vote from home or work must be devised. A national holiday for people to vote is also an interesting concept, meaning that everyone gets the day off from work or school to vote.

The Economy

There seems to be a consensus among economic experts that the mortgage crisis is what caused the economy to crash in 2008, which then led to massive unemployment. Starting in the 1990s there was a political movement, backed by governmental institutions, to encourage Americans to own homes. It became a big national priority for Americans to own homes. Before that time an individual had to have a good credit rating and enough cash to put for a down payment, usually 10–20%, to qualify for a mortgage. So if it was a national mandate for more Americans to own homes, the prerequisite of a good credit rating and down payment would have to be eased. In the spirit of this the sub-prime mortgages came into existence and were extended to borrowers who did not have good credit or cash for a down payment. Basically, an individual with a shady credit ranking and little or no money to put down for a home was given a mortgage regardless. The borrowers were not the only people benefiting from this new type of mortgage. The lenders gave mortgages to risky borrowers in the form of adjustable rate mortgages (called "arm"). An arm was a loan where the bank, based on its own discretion, had the right to change the interest rate. Before the advent of these types of loans, if you had good credit and the money for a down payment you would have a fixed interest rate mortgage, for example a thirty year 9% interest rate. These new arm loans put the borrower at great risk.

After some years these risky borrowers started to default on a massive scale and foreclosure rates increased at an alarming rate. Because of this in 2007 the worldwide economic markets crashed and unemployment soared. Mortgage failures and mass foreclosures caused a global recession due to mortgage bonds.

When someone wants to buy a home, he or she has go to the bank to get a loan, a mortgage, to buy the home. The home is the collateral for the loan. If someone does not pay the loan, banks have the right to foreclose and take the property back. In the 1980s mortgage bonds came into existence. What this means is that if a bank gives out 100 mortgages and needs cash it can sell mortgages in the form of mortgage bonds. Those banks would sell the bonds to traders on Wall Street for example. The way it worked is that if I am a banker who gives out an 8% mortgage for 30 years and then I need cash immediately, I could sell the mortgage as a bond and get maybe 75 cents on the dollar. Then a trader on Wall Street would own the mortgage and trades it as if it were a stock. If interest rates go down, this bond becomes more valuable and can be traded at a higher price. If interest rates go up the bond becomes less valuable. Millions of mortgages throughout the U.S. were being bought and sold, basically as equities, by financial institutions throughout the world. When the mortgage crisis hit, these bonds lost a tremendous amount of value. Banks that held these mortgages as assets could not sustain the economic hit the relatively worthless mortgage bonds caused. Imagine that you own Apple stock. One day it is worth $100 and the next day it is worth $1. This is what happened to financial institutions throughout the world and this is what caused the economic collapse.

There is a simple solution to these problems that will ensure that they never happen again. Mortgage bonds should be illegal. Mortgages should just be between banks and homeowners. Mortgages were never meant to be assets that were traded at financial institutions. The troubling aspect of it all is that Congress actually paid subsidies to banks to make the selling of bonds more attractive. Sub-prime mortgages should also be made illegal. In light of the recent economic meltdown, there should be very strict standards set on all mortgages in the United States. I have devised a new mortgage arrangement that should apply to all mortgages in the United States.

The maximum value of all mortgages, minus a mandatory 20% down payment, would only be two times the gross household income of the borrowers. For example if I make $200,000 per year in gross income and I want to buy a $500,000 home, first I would have to put down $100,000 (which would be the mandatory 20%). Then I would owe $400,000 ($500,000-$100,000=$400,000) on the home. Because that falls in the range of two times my annual gross income ($200,000 x 2=$400,000), I would be able to buy this home following the new rules. There is no cap on how much you can put down on a home. For example, if I wanted to buy a 1.4 million dollar home and I put down 1 million, then under the laws I proposed I would still be able to buy the home because the mortgage would be $400,000 and double of my income.

These measures would have an immediate effect on stabilizing the housing market and the economy. Mortgages should be between the lender and the borrower. When mortgages were invented, this is what the spirit of the concept was. Under the current system sub-prime mortgages and mortgage bonds completely caused the economic crisis in which we find ourselves. People who would put no money down would get adjustable rate income mortgages for houses they could not afford. Then these mortgages would be sold as bonds and classified as assets. When the people with the homes could no longer afford their homes, they defaulted and the bonds lost their value. The property itself, which was supposed to ensure the bond, lost a ton of value because in this climate no one is buying houses and everyone is trying to sell homes.

The reasons why mortgage bonds should be illegal and mortgages have to be regulated using the ways I mentioned are obvious due to what has happened. However because the new mortgage system I have proposed is obviously not the law, for the people that can potentially afford their mortgages we have to find ways to try to keep them in their homes now. Whenever someone who was keeping up with his mortgage payments loses his job, the mortgage should be suspended for 12–18 months until said person finds another job. This should be a federal law. It may seem unfair to the banks, but they gave out a lot of high risk loans to people that had no business owning homes so they should also be punished. Another factor that should be examined is the need to actually own a home for Americans.

Recently, I saw a realty commercial, which said "The dream of home ownership is being threatened". At this point, after everything that has happened, that message seems absurd to me. People do not need to buy homes they cannot afford and go further into debt. What is wrong with renting? Who said that everyone had to own a home? If I did not have much money, I would rent forever and put any extra cash in the stock market, which, in the long run, is proven to give you a much bigger return than owning a home. A house should be seen as a luxury. If you can afford it buy it, not a vital necessity-because it really is not. If people put any extra cash they have in the stock market instead of a home they ultimately cannot afford, imagine the spike the market and economy would get. If a public company gets more money (more investors) that means they can hire more people. The housing market would not necessarily go down, wealthy people could buy up more homes and make money off rent. If we had a rent-based system, everyone wins. The current debt-based system has proven to be bad. A cash-based system is good. In turn, those wealthy homeowners could put their extra money in the market and then we would have a boom. But we live in a country where the government itself stimulates its people to buy homes.

Fannie Mae and Freddie Mac are government-backed entities that were basically formed to make the selling and trading of mortgages as securities easier and to provide security to lenders thereby making it easier for individuals to own homes. For campaigning purposes, politicians artificially stimulated these institutions. They thought that the message that everyone should own a home, regardless of the reality of the solution, was a good campaign slogan. This caused the mortgage bubble to burst, as explained earlier. The message that everyone should own a home and that it is your God given right, is appealing to people who do not know any better. You send out a total populist message like that and you get votes from people that say "yeah me too, I should have a home" even when owning homes is not a real option for many people, or at least the homes they thought they could afford.

Instead of taking logical actions to ameliorate the economy, the main way the government has attempted to fix the economy is by instituting economic stimulus plans. The philosophical concept of a stimulus package is the equivalent of opening up a credit card with a million dollar limit and taking out cash advances of $10,000 per week to buy items that are not vital for your existence. Sure, it will look like you are doing well with nice clothes, an apartment, car, and a fancy lifestyle, but everything is bought in credit and you will pay dearly in the future. The concept of spending your way out of debt, while amassing more debt in the process is backwards and nonsensical. Imagine that you have $100,000 in the stock market and in 2008 it went down to $20,000. If you were a responsible person with a family, would you go and get a loan for $500,000 to re-invest in an attempt to get your money back? I doubt it. If you want to avoid long-term debt, you do not spend your way out of debt, you cut costs and try to save.

The first economic stimulus plan did not work and neither did the second. These plans basically injected taxpayer money into the economy in an effort to create jobs, lower unemployment, and stimulate the economy. Now there are people in the government who are discussing a third. When you continue to take the same actions and you get the same negative results, it is obviously time to change course. What the federal government should do is ask each state for a list of their twenty most pressing infrastructure projects. Then the federal government should choose which ones are worth pursuing based on those lists. This would create jobs and accomplish pressing needs of the states. Instead of one huge stimulus plan, there should be mini-bills that are very specific. The infrastructure bill would just be for infrastructure, and the bill could be written so a high school senior of average intelligence could understand. Instead of bills, like the economic stimulus bill, being so vast and complicated, they should be simplified so Congress knows what they are voting for. The fact that most of Congress did not read the last stimulus bill is appalling. How is this possible? By simplifying the bill, it would ensure that at least more members of Congress would read it.

One reason that these bills are so complex is so members of Congress are able to include pork and ear marks into the bills. Pork and earmarks are special projects in a Congressman's district or a Senator's state. These projects have nothing to do with the economic welfare of the nation and are purely included as political ammunition. For example, if a Congressman is in a district where people want more fish in their waters, when they don't need more fish in their waters, that Congressman could earmark 2 million dollars of the economic stimulus for something as silly as that. This cannot continue. There should be absolutely no pork or pet projects. With specific mini-bills the government could specify exactly where money is going and what jobs are being created. This is something no one seems to know in the current system.

A specific bill addressing the banks would also have to be passed. As far as banks are concerned, the federal government needs to ensure everyone's deposits. At the present time, the federal government ensures everyone up to $250,000. There should be no limits because if you deposit money in a bank the least they can do is keep it safe for you and always available for withdrawal. Giving money to basically bankrupt corporations, to keep them above water is what we should never do. Economic bailouts are just as absurd as economic stimulus packages.

The definition of capitalism is an economic system where everything having to do with the wealth is made and maintained by private individuals or corporations.

The government should not interfere with capitalism in any way. This is the system that the United States has used for years and the system that has made us the strongest economic power in the world. In a capitalist system, all that matters is the bottom line. If a business is failing, capitalism dictates that the business should fail. This should not feel like such a foreign concept. Government bailouts are strictly at odds with the capitalist way. It is useful to think of capitalism like natural selection. For economic evolution to take place, there must be survival of the fittest; the strongest companies thrive and the weakest companies die. Any intervention in this process to save the weak makes the economic species weaker as a whole. Letting failing businesses fail leads to real competition, economic evolution, and innovation. The electronics industry is an example of this. For most of the 1980s the Japanese had the lion's share of the electronics market. Their products flourished. However, one day an American company, Apple, invented the ipod and changed the entire landscape of music and the way it is sold. Apple was required to invent and make something better than what was currently available. A truly capitalist system is very fertile ground for innovation. If the government comes in and bails out huge companies that are failing what happens to the motivation for innovation? Why should I make something better than the competition if the government is going to come in and save the weaker competition? It makes no sense.

The current economic policies will lead to hyperinflation. Economic stimulus plans and bailouts require the printing and spending of money you do not have and extending credit, with no savings to back up the credit. These practices devalue the dollar on a de facto basis. The only good that comes out of this is that the United States gets to be a bad debtor and lose its economic integrity with the rest of the world. Hyperinflation causes the dollar to be worth nothing, thus making our debt worth nothing. For example, if you owe a friend a $100 today and in a year the $100 is worth 50% less than what it was originally, paying him off is not a problem. Using the same rationale, if we owe the Chinese billions of dollars, hyperinflation will make the debt much easier to pay off. Almost the same exact thing happened in Argentina in the 80s and 90s. If this occurs there will be much more damage than losing our economic dignity as a country. Although the relative worth of debt will be decreased, your savings will be worth nothing as well. If a loaf of bread costs $2.00 today, with hyperinflation it could cost $5.00 in a year. Using the same rationale, if you have 100K in the bank and in stocks, it would be worth much less in the future with hyperinflation. For the American individual there is only one defensive play in this type of economic climate and that is to buy commodities, specifically gold, silver, and platinum. These types of commodities, especially gold, maintain and grow their worth in times of hyperinflation.

What our government needs is cash. Not loans from China and not printing more money, new sources of government revenue. We could privatize the U.S. post office, by selling it to a private corporation to run. Privatizing of government institutions is done all the time in other countries to raise cash. With the advent of email the post office is not as important as it was before, sell it and immediately generate a large amount of cash. You could do the same for state revenue by privatizing the Department of Motor Vehicles. Private entities usually do a better job than the government anyway, so our citizens would get better service as a side effect. There are many other possibilities of entities we could privatize, and these two may not be the best but they are just more examples of how we can generate cash, to pay off our debt.

However, further actions need to be taken to ameliorate the economy. As I will discuss in the next section, marijuana and prostitution should be legalized, and both would be taxed at a very high rate. Also amnesty should be given to all illegal aliens and their income should be taxed (this matter will be discussed in full in the "Minorities" chapter). The social security age should be raised. Try looking at raising the retirement age this way: 50 years ago average life expectancy was around 65 years old, now for our generation it is probably around 85 years old and it keeps on going up for younger generations (due to medical advancements), therefore it makes economic sense for people to work longer if they will live longer. The Medicare eligibility age should be raised, for the same rationale to increase the age of social security.

Medicare for approximately the top 2% of the tax bracket should be cut temporarily. I don't like to punish people for being successful, but we are in extreme circumstances. Social security should be temporarily suspended for the top 5% tax bracket (again same rationale). Defense spending should be cut and we should switch from a man-power military, to a futuristic air power and special forces type of army, change from the invasion model to a limited specific surgical operations model. Many military bases from around the world should be shut down and the U.S. should get out of Afghanistan. We should also take a very serious look at foreign economic aid and cut it, across the board, by a certain same percentage, for every country, so it is fair.

Also the government should make all pork spending in legislation illegal-get rid of all the special projects and pork spending once and for all. We should eliminate the estate tax, cut capital gains taxes, and cut the corporate tax rate. This will allow descendants of the deceased to use that extra money to spend more, more capital gains means that the money would be re-invested or spent, and if corporations have more money they will spend more and hire more people (or at least not fire anyone because corporate taxes are so high). All of these factors would stimulate the economy. I would also deregulate corporations in a major way, I know some will say that is how the economic meltdown all started-and that is a fair criticism-but to me Fannie Mae and Freddie Mac caused all of this by stimulating people to get mortgages they could not afford, that is the source of all the problems and to me everything else is a side effect of that. Most anti-trust laws should be repealed, like it or not, corporations should be allowed to run wild if they are not causing malice to the public. New harsh laws need to be passed regarding who qualifies for a mortgage and who does not and how much you have to put down. A law should be passed that ensures that a mortgage can only be between an individual and the lender, meaning the lender cannot sell mortgages to other banks or entities as securities. All the regulations on corporations should not be cut. The ones that make sense to protect the public should be left alone and possibly expanded, but many of the regulations are just ridiculous and they only have the effect of hindering American companies and giving an unfair advantage to other countries, especially China. China is becoming a threat to replace us as the strongest economy in the world. They think they can own us by buying our debt. One way to combat that is by using a lot of the private money in our country. Laws should be passed to make it very attractive for our richest Americans to buy stock in Chinese companies. By doing this we would be combating them by having private Americans with some type of control in their companies.

Marijuana and Prostitution

Everyone in the U.S. wants more government benefits for programs such as healthcare, but no one wants to pay higher taxes. Usually all politicians can do is either not provide the benefit or raise taxes. There is another way. We must change our laws to make relatively harmless things legal that are currently illegal. That way we can tax things that have previously been illegal and we can save government money that was previously spent on prosecuting these crimes. Any offense that we decriminalize must be a relatively harmless offense. Two relatively harmless crimes that we can decriminalize are marijuana possession and prostitution.

Currently the U.S. government spends approximately between 7.5 and 10 billion dollars a year on marijuana prosecutions and arrests. The effects of marijuana are probably less dangerous than the effects of alcohol. Therefore, we would not be making society any more dangerous. People who want to use marijuana can get it from dealers ranging from a 13 year old punk to an old hippie. The illegality of marijuana is not a deterrent. If someone wants to do it, they will. If we legalize it, we will save billions of dollars a year just on the police activity. Furthermore, we could tax it and make more billions. The states of Colorado and Washington recently legalized it, as California has lately, these developments are promising. The money generated from legalization nation wide would go towards government programs. The only people that would be adversely affected are drug dealers. Their revenue would now go directly to the government. If marijuana were legalized many jobs would be created as well. Farmers and tobacco companies would grow it in the United States.

The same mentality applies to prostitution. Currently the average American city spends 7.5 million dollars on prostitution arrests and prosecutions. People that want prostitutes can simply use the internet to get them. Again, people that want to do it, will. With the use of condoms, prostitution is relatively safe. If it is legalized, it could be regulated and taxed to create further government revenue. The government could also provide psychological evaluations for the women to ensure that they fully understand what they are doing, and test the women for AIDS and other sexually transmitted diseases, effectively making them and the people that use prostitutes safer. We would take money away from pimps and make it harder for young American women to be exploited. Again, criminals would be out of business and the government would collect revenue.

By taxing and regulating the use of marijuana and prostitution, and saving all the revenue from prosecution and arrests related to both, the U.S. government would generate tens of billions of dollars. The revenue could be used directly for a prescription drug benefit for Medicare and towards a national health care plan. Or at least the extra money could be used for catastrophic insurance for everyone, this is the most expensive health care cost and we have to start somewhere. It could also be split to give Americans a gas benefit, if oil prices continue to choke the country. The possibilities on what could be done with the funds are endless. The only restriction I would put on the revenue is that it must be used to directly benefit American citizens. None of it would go to the military or anything of that nature.

There is no way that we can rid our society of marijuana and prostitution. They are permanent fixtures. The fact that we are legalizing marijuana and prostitution does not mean that we are saying that they are right or that we want to increase their use at any relevant level. For example, my brother does not drink alcohol, use drugs, or smoke cigarettes. If marijuana is legal he will not go to the drug store and start using it. Strong people that do not use substances will not start simply because of legality. If after a couple of years marijuana or prostitution use skyrockets, which is highly unlikely, decriminalization of both can be repealed.

Health Care

The price of health care is skyrocketing in excess of the inflation rate. The system and the malpractice crisis encourage the ordering of unnecessary tests. Greed encourages unnecessary elective surgery. Medical schools and residency programs are simply not addressing these issues. Government or private subsidies to medical school and training programs should encourage the graduation of more primary care physicians to ensure accessibility and unclog the emergency rooms. As it stands now, people mainly wait until they are really injured or sick and they go to the emergency room instead of seeing primary care physicians on a regular basis. If people went to their primary care physicians more there would be much more preventative care and less last minute emergency medical situations. However this is not the only problem.

There has been an increase in the number of malpractice suits and the amount of the rewards for anguish and suffering. This has led to physicians practicing defensive medicine including an inordinate number of tests and x-rays ordered in offices and emergency rooms. This leads to difficult access to primary care offices, which in turn leads to a number of patients seeking primary care at the hospital emergency rooms. The wait in emergency rooms is anywhere from three to five hours.

There is a lack of medical insurance coverage for 20 percent of the population. The other 80 percent have medical insurance through their employer, Medicaid, or Medicare, but some do not have safety nets for catastrophic illnesses or chronic illnesses. Most commercial insurance companies will drop the patient after one million dollars has been spent on the patient's behalf. Most insurance companies do not cover mental health or do cover mental health to a very limited degree. Insurance companies only partially cover prescription medications. Commercial insurers can pick and choose and refuse to insure patients for previously diagnosed medical conditions and drop patients for catastrophic illnesses. They can dictate which tests are covered and which are not and which modalities of therapies are covered and which are not. The United States is either number one or two in the amount of money that it spends on health care, and yet it is in the twenties when it comes to the quality of the care received. More and more care is delivered by specialists in the U.S. because of the scarcity of primary care physicians. This has been shown to decrease overall quality and increase cost.

Another factor that increases cost is medical malpractice lawsuits. Recently a personal injury attorney, of all people, ran for President and proposed a health care plan. This is ironic because one reason health care is so expensive is because of personal injury lawsuits. Because of the lawsuits, physicians have to pay large amounts in medical malpractice insurance costs and they conduct many unnecessary tests on patients to protect themselves.

In order to afford their malpractice costs, doctors have to raise prices on the services they provide. Ultimately the people paying for these outrageous medical malpractice rewards are the patients. One way to ease these malpractice costs, and give the patients and doctors some relief, would be a federal cap on punitive damages for physicians. When a doctor is sued, he is sued for two different things: punitive damages and economic loss. Punitive damages are pain and suffering and economic loss is literally the money that the person will lose because of the doctor's mistake. For example, imagine that a man is a construction worker. He has to have surgery on his arm and during this surgery the doctor shreds his biceps and triceps. As a consequence the construction worker can no longer work construction. The court would figure out the amount of money that the construction worker would have made for the rest of his life working in construction. That amount is economic loss and justified. Punitive damages are pain and suffering. This is an intangible amount and juries can make it any number, for example for this case they could make it any number from 1 million dollars to 20 million dollars. There are no limits.

Under my plan, economic loss would be left alone and there would be a cap on punitive damages. Furthermore, health insurance companies should provide malpractice insurance to every doctor, because they are benefiting the most from the current health care system. CEOs of medical insurance companies take home millions of dollars in salaries every year. Only 1/3 of premiums go to medical care. 93% percent of health care costs go to patients that are sick. That means that only 7% goes to patients who maintain their health, with visits for things such as physicals and yearly exams. If more people went to physicians more frequently for routine exams the cost of health care would obviously go down. Diseases and other problems would be caught and treated earlier and cheaper.

Another problematic statistic is that 25% of Americans use 2/3 of health care. What we need to do, starting at a young age, is to promote the general wellness of the population so they get sick less frequently and we save more money. However, this will probably not happen as the least qualified people are dictating health care policy. Attorneys in Washington (Congressmen and Senators) should not be the ones deciding what health care policy should be. It would be like doctors changing the legal system and changing laws. Because doctors obviously know a lot more about medical care than attorneys, they should be the ones advising on policy. Hillary Clinton's failed plan led to hundreds of people working on reform, but hardly any physicians were on her team.

Every American should have catastrophic insurance. Catastrophic insurance would be a dollar amount that goes beyond some percentage of an individual's net value. For example, if a person's medical costs go above 40% (or any other percentage that makes sense) of his net worth, this would be considered catastrophic for him.

Money from this program will come from taking away social security, from Americans in the top 5% of the tax bracket, and Medicare from Americans in the top 2% of the economic tax bracket. I hate to punish people for being successful. It is something that does not sit well with me and goes against my fundamental belief system. However, I do not want any of my policies to increase taxes on the American middle class and I understand that government programs cannot be created without creating new revenue. This is why the marijuana and prostitution programs that were previously mentioned are so important. They are new dynamic ways of creating revenue. The revenue that the cuts in benefits, the prostitution tax, and the marijuana tax would generate would probably be more than enough to cover the catastrophic insurance alone. The poorest Americans and our seniors already have it through Medicaid and Medicare respectively. Medicaid is a government program that covers all the medical costs of the poorest Americans and Medicare is a government program that covers the cost of senior citizens.

We have the best physicians and medical technology in the world. If we socialize the system the most competent Americans will not continue going to medical schools and we will be stuck with mediocre doctors. In the foreign countries that have socialized health care many of you may not know that there are private doctors and hospitals-that have nothing to do with the government. Anyone that has money either goes there or comes to the U.S. How many people in this country do you know who have died as a direct consequence of not having health insurance? I do not know any. In one of my medical school interviews a doctor asked me if I was "king of the world" what I would do about health care in this country. I presented him with the question I just asked you. He did not really have a decent answer. Medical schools should just increase the class size by 20%. In a civilized society there should be just as many doctors as lawyers. Honestly what does it say about a society when we have more lawyers than all of Western Europe combined, and I am guessing here but lawyers probably outnumber doctors more than 100 to 1 in this country. We are more interested in protecting our money and making money from others, or in the alternative, in legally challenging other people than our health.

We need to wake up. Notice how we are more than willing to pay for attorneys and no one is saying that legal help should be a right and free. Why don't we socialize legal care as well? Why shouldn't that be free? Public defenders are the equivalent of free clinics so let's not count them. The reason this issue is never brought up is because the overwhelming majority of politicians are lawyers. Shouldn't a single mother on welfare have access to a great family attorney that can get her child support? Why should she have to pay out of her own pocket for that? Doesn't she have a right to get money from her husband to help raise her children? She absolutely does. If she were to use free government resources, she would have to wait forever and go through much red tape. Many impoverished mothers do not even bother. However, when it comes to health care, ineffective politicians are clamoring that everyone deserves it for free. I am against free health care for everyone and free legal care for everyone. But fairness is one of my guiding principles, so if we have a system where health care is socialized, legal care should be as well.

We do not need to change our entire system and let the government ruin it to suit the 20% that do not have health care. What we need is an elective tax for anyone that does not have insurance. If they want insurance, they can pay a higher tax to the federal government and they would get the equivalent of Medicaid. Not much change is needed because Medicaid is already set up. Sell it cheap to these 20%. If we must change our health care program, we should look to programs in Europe that provide universal coverage. Possible solutions are government-run comprehensive medical insurance programs, like Canada, or commercial insurance that would be closely supervised and regulated by the government, like Germany, France and Switzerland. Again, it is with the understanding that the entire population needs to be covered and the insurance companies are strictly regulated by government agencies. The most desirable program would be to follow the European model. Germany, Switzerland and to some extent France have comprehensive universal medical coverage run by private insurers and strictly regulated by the government. All medical expenses, including medications, are covered one hundred percent. The insurance companies do not have the right to refuse anyone or drop anyone. Patients choose their own physicians. The social and mental health programs are also covered under this umbrella. Patient satisfaction in those countries is extremely high. Healthcare in those countries has, however, come at a high cost. In Germany eight percent of every worker's salary is contributed to the insurance fund. The employer contributes a similar amount. This is to say that if an individual makes one thousand dollars a month or one million dollars a month eight percent of that amount is withheld for the insurance fund. However, people that believe that Europe or Canada has better health care programs than we do, just because it's free, do not realize that patients wait months to get vital procedures and Canadians and Europeans that have money often come to the U.S. to get treatment.

Education and Beyond

The number one problem facing troubled public schools today is a complete lack of discipline. A school's main responsibility is educating students and keeping them alive. When it comes to the personal safety of students, schools cannot fail; there is absolutely no margin for error. School shootings in particular stem from a complete lack of discipline. Order must be instilled in troubled public schools. School shootings only happen in public schools because private schools have discipline and they do not have to deal with silly government restrictions on discipline.

A teacher's job is to teach in a quiet harmonic environment. But, teachers need partners. Everyone does. Parents are those partners and they must help kids with homework and actively participate in their kids' education. There is no magic about it. Studying is hard work. About 90% of kids are born with the same intelligence level, it is a question of developing it and parents and teachers must work together. In school there should be very little tolerance for bad behavior. But again, teachers alone cannot accomplish the goal of providing discipline because they need assistance.

Because there is a higher incidence of violence in inner city public schools, retired police officers should be working security on site. There should be at least one per every one hundred students. These police officers could carry beepers and teachers would have emergency buttons on their desks that signaled the beepers. In exchange for 5 years of service, the government could waive the estate tax for these officers. Also, as further incentive, offer scholarships to state schools for up to 3 grandchildren or children of these retired police officers.

Another measure of security for inner city and non inner city schools would be mandatory drug testing for every student. These tests would take place once a month on random days. Some may say that this is a violation of a student's civil liberties. But what rights would the school really be violating? Students have absolutely no right to be on drugs while in school, therefore there is no right being violated by testing them. The testing would be done for the public welfare and safety of other students and teachers. If any trace of drugs is found in their system, the students get one warning and a one-week suspension. The reason the students would not be treated more harshly is because the parents should be given a chance to handle the problem. However, two strikes and you are out. The penalty for failing two drug tests in one year would be expulsion for one year.

I suggest implementing expulsions more liberally for issues including, but not limited to, drug use. If a student is expelled twice, meaning he returns the following year and is expelled again, he should be sent to boot camp style reform schools. This would create a much needed deterrent to acting out in class. Too often inner city schools are becoming day care centers and the teachers are basically glorified babysitters. Another issue that many do not think about is that problem students make it more difficult for students that actually want to learn. If teachers are constantly scared and distracted how will they be able to teach effectively?

Teachers at inner city schools must be paid more money. If you pay teachers more money, more people will become educators and this will increase the amount of talented teachers. Classroom size can be increased if you have better teachers with the aforementioned security. Larger classrooms cut costs. If teachers are making more money, they should also be tested academically on a regular basis. Only capable teachers should be rewarded. Teachers would be required to pass annual exams on the subjects that they teach. Only teachers that take and pass these tests would be paid more money. But some students need more than just great teachers for support.

Inner city schools should have on site psychiatrists. These psychiatrists will have to work on a voluntary basis, as public schools have no additional government means of paying them. We can offer partial scholarships to medical school students that are planning on pursuing a career in psychiatry in exchange for a 5 hour per week commitment for four years. This would approximately represent fair value for the scholarship I have in mind. Public schools could also try to attract retired psychiatrists. These psychiatrists would only speak to very troubled children who would otherwise have no other access to care.

Because people in wealthy areas pay higher taxes they have more resources than inner city schools. This is simply not fair. For instance, these affluent students have computers at home and at school. Many might be thinking that inner city education is not their problem, but it is. The public pays the taxes to keep poor people on welfare. I truly believe that stereotypes that state that certain minorities are lazy or stupid are absurd. They must be given a chance and the current system does not afford low-income minorities that. I was a student at the most diverse medical school in the country and I can assure you that minorities, when given a chance, are neither lazy nor less capable than anyone. If their educational conditions are changed more will become contributing members of society and not only will welfare costs go down, but our nation will be tapping more of its resources. We need to tap every resource that we have. For students to unleash their full potential, adjustments must be made to school curriculum as well. High schools should offer public computer trade schools or liberal arts high schools. If a student has no intention of going to college there should be trade schools that would accommodate his or her needs. After having a trade school education, young people would be able to join the work force immediately. Currently students who do not go on to college are only qualified to take the lowest paying jobs. This is simply not acceptable.

Curriculum for a liberal arts school would be English, History, Science, and Math. One semester each for Art and Music would be required as well. Foreign Language would be offered as an after school elective that would not be required. These are the important courses that every school should have. Art and music stimulates the brain to succeed academically and is therefore essential. Athletics is also vital. Every student should be required to play a sport. This is a good idea because sports instill discipline and they show students that being part of a team is often more effective than doing things alone. Also, being part of a sports team provides a great sense of friendship.

A high school investment class would be offered as an after school elective. Too often people in society either have no knowledge of the way our stock market works or they learn years after high school. The stock market has been proven to give investors the most return out of any other investment avenue and we must therefore teach our children about it. Teachers could be financial planners from the area or local college students who are economic majors who could teach the class for college credit. This would give the kids a solid understanding of how the market works, and a healthy tool on how to make money. The students would buy and sell stocks, with fake money, in the first year and do the same for the second year. The schools could have contests with prizes that go towards the college education of students that do really well in the class.

A common sense approach would also be used in teaching the other elective class foreign language. When a human being learns their native language, as toddlers, they learn to speak before they learn to write. So teaching how to write at the same time as you teach how to speak makes no sense. For example, no one teaches babies how to write at the same time they teach them how to speak. Therefore, schools need to teach students how to speak first and only after they have a solid command on the language should the school introduce writing. We should start teaching foreign languages in first grade.

Also starting at a very young age we should teach self-defense for women and martial arts or boxing for men. This would ensure that children at a very young age would have a physical outlet to burn calories and be fit while learning to defend themselves. Currently many parents are failing at providing physical fitness for their children, and the result is a child obesity epidemic. We must begin to attack this problem. Just as kids who are failing academically take summer school, kids who are failing physically should go to a boot camp style summer program that gets them in shape. Children that are at the bottom 25th percentile in weight for their height would go to boot camp. This would teach them that it is wrong to be so overweight and it would get them in shape early in their lives. They would also be forced to take intensive nutrition courses so they know what they are doing to themselves when they eat garbage and to let them know what the specific healthier options are. The plan would eventually save money for health care. These high-risk people are what make national health care costs skyrocket. A fit America is an integral part of saving healthcare. However, being physically fit is only half the problem, children must also be mentally fit. Another idea that would save young lives in a more direct manner is increasing the driving age.

Because high schools teach driver's education they would be integral in enforcing this type of law. According to Allstate insurance motor vehicle crashes are the number one cause of death for teens in America. They take nearly 6,000 young lives and injure another 300,000 teens every year. There is a simple way to deal with this problem. The legal minimum driving age should be increased from sixteen years old to eighteen years old. This idea would reduce these deaths by approximately fifty-percent. Since the current minimum driving age is sixteen that means that sixteen, seventeen, eighteen, and nineteen year olds are the only teenagers that can legally drive. If the minimum driving age is raised, that means that only eighteen and nineteen year olds would be driving. Consequently, half of teenagers would be off the roads. There really is no reason for sixteen and seventeen year olds to have licenses anyway. Although it takes a small burden away from the parents who drive their kids around, the main reason for it seems to be for kids to go to parties and for dating, neither of those is a major national concern. Judging by where we rank compared to educational systems across the world, it is optimal that students worry less about socializing and more about academics. That way we can get more young Americans in college.

Every high school graduate that wants to should be pursuing higher education at this point in our history. Not being able to afford college should not be an issue, although it currently is. When politicians who are for socializing health care bring up that health care is free in Europe and it works there, what they fail to mention is that in all those European countries higher education is basically free. In the U.S. we have to pay anywhere from $30,000 (the absolute cheapest) to $70,000 per year for graduate school. Socialize education first and then worry about health care. Isn't education a fundamental right as well? Who arbitrarily made high school the limit of free education in this country and why did they stop there? When they did that, say 100 years ago, a high school education was equivalent to what a college education is now (as far as how valuable it is in the workplace). We have a debt-based society and our current system is designed to leave students who pursue a college degree in a large amount of debt. If individuals want a house, they have to go in debt. If students want to go to college or be a lawyer or doctor, they have to go in debt. If people did not have school debt to pay off (like they do not in Europe) maybe they would be able to actually afford their healthcare, or they would be able to pay higher taxes for universal healthcare. The only people that do not go into debt are the rich, who pay in cash, so the system perpetuates the rich staying rich. How many more people would go to college and beyond if it was free? Within one generation we would have a much more educated population ready to solve our problems with solutions more creative than just spending and raising taxes. America would be investing in the development of the American people. In twenty years, I want every American to have a graduate degree. Education can change the world. Unemployed Americans now need to do anything they can to educate themselves. If someone does not have too much money, they can take online classes. If someone has money but they lost their job, go get a graduate degree. Do something worthwhile when you have time on your hands. Do not look at it like you are changing careers (you could quit the extra education when you find a job) look at it like expanding your knowledge base.

I understand that socializing education is a huge project that will probably not happen any time soon, but in the mean time changes can be made to make higher learning more efficient. Graduate schools should make it easier to get in programs like medical school, law school, or business school. Expand admissions (get more money) and fire about 50% of the professors and replace their lectures by online lectures (save money). In medical school the smartest students took most lectures online, it's more effective-students can pause and go back if they do not understand something and they can fast forward if they are already familiar with the topic. It is a clearly superior system for most classes. If it is proven to be the most efficient in probably the hardest and most intense educational atmosphere, medical school, it means it is the most efficient system across the board. But again, it is better for most, not all classes. Unemployed professors can become glorified tutors that charge a lot. Depending on how many students they tutor, it could be a wash as far as income. Because the government cannot socialize education overnight, at the very least the government can pay for online college entirely for students that have at least a B average coming out of high school. Any citizen would be eligible. It is better than unemployment because at least it is going somewhere productive. Those students that got the free online college would not be eligible for unemployment.

Changes in between high school and college need to be made to get the most out of our high school students as well. For two years after high school every American should work in a government sponsored civil service program. Many students waste time in their first two years of college using drugs, getting drunk and having sex while under the influence. Many students drop out, others get mediocre grades and this interferes with their dreams. For example, they cannot go to medical or law school because of their bad grades. In the process, the money of the parents or loans they are taking out is being wasted. They change majors because they do not know enough about the reality of the careers they are choosing. About half of students do not end up doing anything related to their majors. With the civil service program, if a student wanted to be a doctor he/she would work in a hospital, if a student wanted to be a police officer he/she would work in a police station, etc. Government would pay the participant a small stipend. With this type of job experience the students would know something about the careers they plan to pursue.

Also a natural consequence of the program would be to give eighteen year olds of different social classes and racial makeup an opportunity to work together and get to know each other, when under normal circumstances they may not. Career private school students would get a chance to meet with people that are outside of their crowd, and career public school students would get the same opportunity. If we want the citizens of our country to work together as a team for the same goal of success, they have to get to know each other to form important bonds such as trust and friendship. Furthermore, they would enter college at the age of twenty-years old, which would make them more mature.

While performing the duties of the civil service, whenever possible, the students would live at home. This would continue to give them a sense of discipline rather than the sense of reckless abandon that often accompanies the college experience. For young people that are already mature and may not need this type of program, it will not hurt. Any experience in one's field of potential interest is useful. Exceptions would be made in these programs for individuals who do not have a GED or the grades for college and want to use the time to enhance their college applications record in local junior colleges and places of that nature.

Minorities

The black community must do better in our society. For many reasons, in terms of poverty and crime, the black community has not collectively made much progress in the last forty years. Fathers that leave their children are one of the biggest problems that affects them. There must be a government agency whose only function is to find fathers that leave their kids, this agency would also find white and Hispanic fathers too, but they would mainly be concerned with the black community because proportionally the numbers are staggering for their demographic.

Once found they would have to spend time with their kids and give them money or it would be a felony and they would automatically go to jail for a minimum of five years. There must be a very real deterrent to black fathers abandoning their children. This will lead to less crime and more advancement for the black minority. A child being raised by a father and a mother makes all the difference. Many black single mothers do not know how to find an attorney to represent them in their pursuit of child support and even if they do they do not have the money. The government should provide the funds necessary to find fathers of abandoned children. Poor fatherless children often turn into criminals or recipients of welfare in their adult lives. If more of these children have both parents in their lives, this will lead to less children growing up into criminals or welfare recipients. Therefore, the government will save funds and new income would also be generated. Children raised by both parents would be productive members of society, in the overwhelming majority of cases kids with two parents do better than kids with one, and the tax money they would contribute would help the government. Most importantly, these children would have the chance to have happy and productive lives.

There are current government programs that attempt to advance minorities in our country but they are flawed. Affirmative action, for example, is one. Affirmative action should be based on economic status, not race. Blacks and Hispanics that need it would still get it but so would low income Caucasians. This would eliminate the prejudice over the issue and allow people that have the most need to matriculate in college. The black community would still get the majority of the spots that affirmative action creates because, unfortunately, proportionally they make up a very large amount of poverty stricken Americans. However, if there are two black people who are doctors and they have a son who has not suffered any disadvantage whatsoever, they would not be given priority status. A white poverty-stricken child, who has the relevant academic background and whose parents are on welfare, would be given the opportunity. Objectively speaking no one can argue that this does not make sense.

We must get rid of double standards. Historically there was a double standard where whites could do or say anything to blacks and not have to suffer any consequences. The way to correct that wrong is not to replace it with another double standard. In the media we can see that when whites say something negative about blacks, whether it is true or not, they are automatically blamed for being racist. However, blacks can say whatever about whites and they are not racists. This is not right. When it comes to the entertainment industry, regarding minorities that are successful and contributing to society in the form of taxes, the establishment meddles in their careers.

Many in the media often state that they find certain explicit types of rap music reprehensible. Rappers may say things that are disturbing to some, but the first amendment must always be respected. Forget about the sanctity of the framers for a second and try to appreciate all of the creative juice that flows from protecting that amendment. Every American benefits from the first amendment in one way or another, whether it is a person voicing his disdain against the American government or a rapper using lewd derogatory language toward women. The way that Americans who do not like this behavior benefit is by engaging in critical thinking and dialogue. America needs this in the same way that a starving man needs a sandwich. Rappers might have lyrics that bother many people, but their children go to good schools and receive an excellent education and I am sure that they have a better chance of becoming productive members of society than children growing up in the ghetto. Furthermore, the artists themselves pay a lot of taxes and are contributing members of society. Calvin Broadus, a.k.a Snoop Dog, a rapper who uses explicit lyrics, for instance, is a model of parenting for the black community. He is a former gang member who lives with his kids, coaches them at football and makes sure they pass their classes. American history is full of examples of people that made their money in unsavory ways and then used it to benefit their children.

Joseph Kennedy made his money by bootlegging alcohol, which at the time was considered as bad as importing illegal drugs now. I think a rapper using lyrics traditional American people think is offensive is not even close to as bad as someone importing illegal drugs, and Kennedy's son was President. If blacks have been poverty-stricken for so long, people should be ashamed to take away a form of music that makes the poorest members of their minority money. I would like to see how much money in taxes the top 20 grossing rappers have paid in the past ten years. If the government or anyone else has that much of a problem with rap lyrics, why has no one suggested that the government give up rappers' tax money and give it to poor black communities instead? The situation changes when it comes to someone taking the government's money away.

As far as misogynistic rap lyrics, the point is that most men, black or white, know that if they want to have sex with a woman they will not reach that goal by insulting her in the worst ways imaginable. None of the current politicians that talk negatively about rap grew up with it and they probably do not own any rap albums. I went to a public high school that was about 30% black, and I know that when my friends and I would repeat rap lyrics with cuss words it would be in a joking manner. An analogous situation can be found in the 1950s hit television comedy the "Honeymooners". Ralph Kramden would threaten to hit his wife and "send her to the moon". I don't remember conservatives or liberals back then wanting to take him off the air because he was threatening to beat his wife. I don't recall hearing about kids beating up girls because of that. That was the most popular show in the U.S. The same is true with rap music. Again, I think threatening to beat up your wife while clenching your fist and screaming "I'll send you to the moon" is objectively worse than insulting a woman with words. Ask any woman if she would rather be threatened physically by a man or insulted verbally. This is the type of tacit form of racism that we must watch out for, not racism against blacks, or other minorities, but racism against words. We are living in a world with terrorism and people get wrapped up in this nonsense. This is the type of behavior that we should eradicate.

Many black professional athletes come from poverty and familial situations where a father is often not around. Living in the streets and growing up fighting and having to constantly think about survival, make many of these individuals aggressive, strong, and talented. All of these attributes are desirable in athletes. However, once they become professionals, leagues like the NFL and NBA expect them to keep the qualities that make them good on the field and develop new qualities off the field. An expensive contract does not automatically make qualities people possess disappear. At this point, the owners and the commissioners treat the players as property instead of as human beings. Whenever trouble arises, especially lately, leagues are not even affording the individual our government's due process. They take measures before the government case is over. Owners and commissioners want the players to respect them; however they treat them like property instead of family. What I mean is if an individual has a son that commits a crime, if you cared about him and were not just concerned about making money from his career, wouldn't he/she hire him an attorney and support him? Instead these leagues suspend players and take actions that are prejudicial. The Mike Vick situation is a perfect example. Vick was a young black quarterback for the Atlanta Falcons who was the face of the franchise. In 2007 he was caught hosting dogfights in his home. Although Vick was the Atlanta Falcons' best player, his team cut ties with him before his case was over. What type of message does that send? The Falcons could not even afford him the respect of waiting until he was tried to cut ties. If players are to respect others, they should also be respected. I personally think what he did to those dogs is unbelievably reprehensible and awful, but I never had a very close relationship with him, as the owners and management of the Atlanta Falcons did, I do not owe him anything. I feel that they do.

Many sportswriters speak about how professional athletes are role models and that is why it is important for them to lead totally morally strong lives. This is not true.

The day of sports role models, like Joe DiMaggio and Babe Ruth, are over. In fact, those guys were committing a lot of improprieties as well but the media didn't follow them around everywhere salivating for them to make mistakes. Drinking was like drug use in the days of prohibition and most athletes were drinking in the good old days. The sports media likes fantasizing about how things were different in the golden era of sports. This too is bogus; in 1918 eight players of the Chicago White Sox were paid to lose in the World Series. Nothing of that magnitude has happened since, in any professional sport in the United States. That put the integrity of baseball as a whole in question, which was the most popular sport in those days. Mike Vick's situation did not do the same for football. What's worse in the eyes of the league, a team throwing a championship or a football player betting on dog fighting?

Back then most kids had harsh relationships with their fathers who were working most of the time. Sports figures were important role models because no one was filling that need. Now kids have mothers and fathers who should be and usually are their role models. The poor black kids that don't have fathers will not stop liking Vick because he is involved in dog fighting, trust me. Compared to what a kid has to go through in the projects that is nothing. All ninety-percent of sports fans really care about is watching the player produce on the field. If he commits a crime, let our criminal system handle it that is why they are there. Everyone deserves due process. For example, if the courts would have found Mike Vick innocent, they did not he was found guilty, the damage done to his image by the NFL would have already occurred. The commissioner suspended him basically stating to the country that he is guilty. Would you have much respect for someone that treated you like that? A white athlete who played the same position for the Pittsburgh Steelers, Ben Reothlisberger, was accused of rape and his team stuck with him throughout the process and he was eventually found not guilty. But the point is that they supported him in his moment of need for a crime that is very serious and also totally reprehensible.

Many athletes and musicians in the black community grow up in housing projects, and the United States is simply failing minorities as far as these projects are concerned. The housing projects in our country are not working. Theoretically, the point of a housing project is for the government to help the poorest people in our society have lives that are as close to normal as possible, thereby helping the residents get back on their feet and move on from the projects to more independent lives. Housing projects should never be looked at as a permanent housing situation. They should be looked at as temporary housing. This would be better for the government, because less money would need to be allocated there, and they could lead better lives. At the very least this type of system needs to ensure the safety of its residents. As the situation stands, housing projects from New York to Philadelphia to Chicago to the South are running rampant with crime. There are several measures that need to be taken to revolutionize the housing project experience. The way we should begin the process is a one housing project at a time mentality.

The blueprint I am about to describe needs to be implemented in one housing project and if it works, then it should replicated and continued. One of the bigger problems with many government programs is that they try new ideas on a grand scale before they see if they work on a small scale. The proper way is the opposite, like how the FDA tests new drugs on a small group before dispersing them to the general public.

The first housing project, we will refer to it as Housing Project "A", would be a 10 floor building with approximately 60 residents. The reason for the small building is that people tend to respect the property and their neighbors more in a smaller setting. If someone knows his/her neighbor personally, it is easier to respect them and if you live in a smaller complex it feels more home like. Next, trees, bushes, and gardens would be planted and the esthetics of the outdoors would be taken very seriously. Medical studies have proven that people are more productive and happy when they are in pleasant environmental settings.

Every resident on welfare would have to perform jobs for the community in order to receive their government paychecks. There are many jobs that people with little or no job experience could perform. They could be cooks, servers, day care providers, tutors, handymen, free clinic employees, or athletic coaches to name a few. This would give a sense of worth to every member of the community. Also they would be receiving job experience that could help them in their future endeavors. Just having a good job recommendation that proves someone is a hard worker and shows up to work on time is very valuable.

These residences would have a constant major police presence. One squad car would be at project A at all times, with back up nearby. No liquor stores would be allowed within five miles of the project. No fast food restaurants would be allowed within five miles of the project as well, heart disease runs rampant in the projects and most people living there are not eating in a healthy way. The children being raised in the projects would have their education monitored closely. From kindergarten to the beginning of high school, in the inner city, we must create huge youth centers for these children. These centers would include tutors, sports, music, art programs and outdoor fields. In order to do any of the fun things (music, sports, or art) the children would be required to spend 2 hrs a day with a tutor. You would be amazed how many results you can get if an elementary school student spends two hours a day with tutors who know what they are doing. Seminars would be designed to try to attract pro athletes, musicians, artists, and successful business people to speak to the youth. Also, for every "A" that a child from the project receives on his report card, the government would reward the parent(s) with $50.00. This may not seem fair to the average taxpayer, but it would be an investment in the future of our country. This will help children, hopefully, take school seriously and become productive members of society. That way there would not be generations of families living in the projects. Projects must be an example of what we ideally want for our citizens who, for whatever reason, cannot fend for themselves. The housing projects must not be a national embarrassment, as they are now.

Illegal activity would not be tolerated in project A. Anyone caught with any amount of drugs, after they served their appropriate sentence, would be required to go to rehabilitation or they would not be allowed back in the project. Any gang activity in the projects would be treated the same way, but if the gang member wanted to come back he would have to complete 100 hours of service for the project. A second offense would result in permanent expulsion from the project. To give innocent kids who want to succeed the proper chance to persevere, nothing that gets in the way of their progress can be tolerated. If the children's parents are the ones getting in the way, a different program must be instituted.

If mothers or fathers are doing a bad job with their kids or if the kids are not getting good grades, the children would be taken away to a type of boarding school, but it would be a governmental boarding school close to the projects where the parents live. That way parents could visit whenever they want and the children would be sent home on weekends. But any parent of a child who was in the government boarding school program would forfeit the right to receive child support from government or it would be greatly reduced. That child support, along with grants and charity, would be the tuition that would go to the school.

While these measures would mainly help impoverished members of the black, Hispanic, and white community, the main issue facing Hispanics is illegal immigration. Something decisive must be done about that.

Immigration

Regardless of what the leadership says in our country nothing is going to happen with immigration. Both sides of the political spectrum have been talking for years about what they want to do yet nothing happens. The real world options are mass deportation or full amnesty and no one is willing to do either. Given those two options, we should accept the reality on the ground and give full amnesty to all illegal aliens. In turn, the federal government could tax their incomes and increase government revenue. After that we would have to take mass action to secure the border. In the alternative we could secure the border first and then grant full amnesty to all illegal aliens that are already here. The illegals are here to stay, whether anyone likes it or not, that is the reality. The issue must be resolved once and for all. I know that theoretically we should not reward bad behavior (people who crossed the border illegally) and punish good legal behavior (people who are following the rules and waiting for their green cards).

I must admit that I respect this argument against amnesty when it comes to immigration. Why should someone that cut in line be ahead of other immigrants who respected the law? That is totally logical and the right argument theoretically. If you are against illegal immigration it does not mean that you are against legal immigration in general. Opponents of cracking down on illegal immigration make it seem like if someone steals a television and if someone else complains about it, that what you are saying is that no one should own a television. However, extreme circumstances call for extreme measures. Sometimes principles need to be compromised for the sake of the country. In these very tough circumstances it is necessary to adjust and address the reality and the solutions that can be unfair. I know that is unfortunate for the people who followed the rules, but that is how I feel about it. When money is the issue it is all about the bottom line, and the bottom line is that full amnesty will create money for the government.

After full amnesty is granted, if the government wants to create jobs, it should hire new agents to secure the borders. This would create needed jobs and it would be a real and worthwhile action. There are ways to secure borders. North Koreans do not freely cross to South Korea as East Germans (when they were a communist closed society) did not freely cross to West Germany. I realize our border is much larger, but at the same time we have more resources than North Korea or East Germany did. We could use the new government revenue, based on taxing everyone that has full amnesty, on employing people to secure the borders. That way, our government money would not be wasted. Some of them may not qualify, based on their incomes, to pay any taxes-but for the ones that do, I would have a flat tax for everyone that is employed, 20% or another percentage that makes sense. If securing the borders is the focus, an effective and inexpensive strategy might be making the border a mine field. I do not like or support that idea. I am just saying that if the goal is to solve a problem, there are always ways, regardless of how ugly they are.

Corporations and the wealthy are the people that really benefit from illegal immigration. Can lower middle-class or lower-class people afford maids, nannies or land-scapers? No, they cannot. Can ordinary people afford fruit-pickers? Absolutely not, but corporations can. They have been breaking the law and taking advantage of Mexicans, and other illegal immigrants, and the govern-ment. The person or company that hires illegals should be prosecuted. By talking to illegals and the entity that hired them, the government should estimate how many hours each illegal worked for the company, or person, and calculate how much minimum wage would have been for all the hours they worked. Subtract the money (below minimum wage) they did get from what they should have been paid (minimum wage). Then give the difference to the government. Look at this as a way for the illegal aliens to pay for past taxes that were never collected.

It is not fair that just because of geographic location Mexicans get to come to our country while others in more desperate situations cannot. Mexico has a stron-ger economy than most Central American countries for instance, and those foreigners (who are also Hispanics) do not have the benefit of immediate proximity, so they cannot come to the U.S., that is not right. These are people who are just as poor and desperate as Mexicans, more so in most cases. Every country in Africa has more people dying of disease and genocide than Mexico. After full amnesty is granted to illegal Hispanics, people who are in the most need in the world should be able to come to the U.S. ahead of Mexicans. The policy that we have is indirectly racist; Mexicans can come in, but other Hispanics, Africans, and many other deserving people cannot. After the borders are secure, people who are experiencing genocide anywhere in the world should get preferential treatment over Mexicans or anyone else that is trying to get in the U.S. There are plenty of people worse off than Mexicans in the world. I want to live in a country that helps people who are potential victims of genocide find a better life. By letting Africans come here, we would not simply be giving them a better standard of life, we would be saving their lives. I can guarantee that the money that they would potentially make in the U.S. would stay in the U.S., opposed to Mexicans that send money made in the U.S. to relatives in Mexico. The African countries where they come from are so corrupt that the citizens know that any money sent home would be stolen. We cannot just randomly help people; we need to help the people that are most in need.

After we grant amnesty to every illegal alien, in the future, every illegal immigrant should be deported; the word deported has become such a politically incorrect buzzword. Supporters of illegal immigration make it seem like when we deport a Mexican to Mexico we are sending them to a death camp. When in reality they are getting a free ride home to a country where they were born, speak the language, and have relatives. Last I checked, in Mexico, there is no genocide against Mexicans.

Anyone who is given a visa from any country, especially Mexico, should be required to pass an elementary school level oral English test.

We should offer automatic citizenship for any member of the Western Hemisphere who agrees to serve in the military for three years.

Penal and Judicial System

Our penal system is completely unacceptable for a civilized society. Theoretically, prisoners are the worst that our society has to offer. They are people who cannot follow the rules of our society. To "rehabilitate" these criminals we send them to prisons that are cesspools and worse than the outside world. We live in a country where guards beat and torture American citizens in American jails and fellow inmates rape and attack other inmates on a daily basis. Drugs run rampant in our jail system. If these people are criminals in the normal world, which is much cleaner, safer, and less violent, what will they be in American jails, where the conditions are much worse? A disproportionate amount of inmates who have to suffer these injustices are black. In light of all of this, it is particularly grotesque that so much attention is put on how we treat foreign detainees who may or may not be terrorists. What does that say about our society? Instead, we should be concerned more about our own citizens, many potentially innocent, who are in jail. The worst aspect is that no one cares.

The reason this administration and prior administrations could not care less about American citizens who are in jail is that there is no political gain in making conditions better in our jails. Whose vote would be gained if our penal system was improved? Before investigating how we treat would be foreign terrorists, we should investigate and completely cleanse our own jail system. Currently, it is a disgrace. The best way to judge a society on a human rights basis is to investigate its jail system, a writer, Dostoyevsky, said that. How does getting beaten and raped rehabilitate criminals and make them ready to join society again? Even simple measures like installing video cameras all over jails would make a world of difference. An independent justice commission could review the tapes from the video cameras. The fact that no one cares about American minority inmates, but yet they care a lot about foreign inmates, that may be terrorists, demonstrates how warped the values of politicians have become. Improving conditions in our jails is never a national issue and that is disgraceful. If political correctness is the focus, we should stop worrying about trivial matters such as whether "black" or "African American" is the right term when you refer to them, and help minorities when no one else will. Regarding American inmates, our society is so simple minded that the only national issue America seems to care about is the death penalty. What about everything that happens in between incarceration and death? That is what a human life is for inmates.

There needs to be a uniform system that dictates what inmates should do while they are in jail. Every member of the jail community should be working eight hours a day. Eat, sleep, work, watch tv, and read is all they should be doing. They should be given books and allowed to watch minimal television for entertainment. There should be no computer access whatsoever, as criminal operations can be easily conducted online. If anyone is caught in a jail selling drugs, or getting in a fight they should be in solitary confinement. One way to help enforce these changes is to increase the amount of guards. It is also common knowledge that many guards are corrupt and violate the prisoners' rights constantly. Again, no one seems to care about that.

I have first-hand knowledge of police officer and prison guard violations of prisoners' rights. In June of 2008, I was pulled over because I was speeding. The police officer had not clocked me and therefore had no proof that I was speeding. He asked me where I was coming from, I was coming from a friend's home and I did not want to involve anyone else in this situation so I said it was not relevant where I was coming from. This angered the police officer. He and his partner handcuffed me and made me wait in the back of a squad car. Soon after, his partner "found" a crack cocaine pipe in my car with crack residue, I saw the partner put the crack pipe in my car. At this point it is fundamental to point out that I have never done crack cocaine in my life and neither has anyone that I know. Furthermore, I had never had, in my possession, a crack cocaine pipe. Soon after my arrest I took a blood test and a urinalysis that came up negative for cocaine and corroborated my innocence.

The three possibilities of who put that crack pipe in my car are someone who randomly walked to my car when it was parked and put a crack pipe in it (highly unlikely), the people that park my car at home (also highly unlikely because they have never left anything in my car for the past twenty years), or the police officer planting the pipe in my car (which I saw him do). The police did not have anything legitimate to arrest me for; they didn't clock me driving fast so they didn't have proof of my speeding and they obviously took the response to where I was coming from as disrespectful to them. Therefore they planted drugs in my car. This was the first in a series of completely unacceptable actions taken against me by supposed guardians of the peace in a civilized society.

I was then taken to a police station in Chicago and the arresting officer began questioning me. During the questioning after the police did not let me make a phone call, a series of officers came into the room where I was. This is a sample of the questions that they were asking: "Who do you think will win the Presidential election?", "Do you like the work that Mayor Daley is doing in the city of Chicago?" Those questions obviously had nothing to do with the reason I was arrested.

From the police station I was taken to the Cook County, IL jail. There I was held for total of about 36 hours. During this entire time, including the original police station, I was not allowed to use the telephone and I was rarely given water to drink. I, along with mostly black arrestees, was taken from jail cell to jail cell in what I gather was a poor excuse for a processing system. No one told us what was going on, and when the corrections officers did speak to us, they would yell at us and use profanity. They treated us like animals. At this stage we were supposedly innocent until proven guilty in the eyes of the law. They made us take off our socks and walk around barefoot. I am not sure what the point of that was, the only thing that happened as a result of this was my feet being cut and blistered. My 36-hour stay included a "psychological" evaluation. During this time the jail employees were writing numbers on our forearms with markers. I did not understand why they did that; maybe it was a form of identification.

The corrections officers asked me my religion, my dad's religion, my mother's religion, whether I've ever dressed up as a woman, and whether I was a homosexual. I told them my parents' religions and obviously said no to the last questions. I felt like I was in a third world country and not a democratic state. I again asked for the telephone and water and they said no. Because I could not take it anymore, I spoke up. I stated that they were wasting my time, and they were treating all of the other inmates as if they were not human beings. I explained to the guards that what they were doing was a clear violation of my human rights. The corrections officer didn't like this type of talk, so he came into the cell and pushed me. I fell backwards. Next another corrections officer came in the room and started screaming at me. He told me that if I didn't stop complaining he would "kick my ass up and down the jail". This comment was designed to frighten me. This man grabbed my shirt with both his hands and proceeded to drag me down the cell to an individual cell. At this point I stopped talking.

After staying in solitary the guards took me to the hospital. There the doctors ran some tests and then I was sent to the holding area of Cook County Jail. During my stay at the jail, I again asked to use the phone and finally the next day they led me to two public phones. Both of the public phones were out of order. When I complained about this, I was beaten by the corrections officers and put in solitary confinement. Hours after the beating, my family, with the help of the State's Attorney and the FBI, found me and got me out. I was taken to the hospital where a urinalysis revealed that there were no drugs in my system. The hospital determined that I was dehydrated from the lack of water.

All of the charges against me were subsequently dropped. Also, I was later asked by a former police officer if there was going to be a lawsuit on my part against the city of Chicago. I decided not to take any action. Taxpayers are who would have paid the cost for the lawsuit. I am against taxpayers having to pay for lawsuits. But, I also believe in fighting back when wronged, therefore I will do everything in my power to report my ordeal to higher authorities. One month after I was arrested the U.S. Department of Justice wrote a scathing report about all of the problems with Cook County Jail. This was reported in the Chicago Sun-Times and the Chicago Tribune (Chicago's biggest and most widely read newspapers). They corroborated everything that I said. The report discussed arbitrary beatings, insults, and inmate suicides due to lack of proper medication, not giving inmates with psychological problems their proper medications, illegal questioning, and other infractions. They stated that if the

Cook County Jail did not change their ways that the Department of Justice would sue them.

After being arrested I fully realized that if this was happening to me, it must happen to people all the time, especially defenseless poor black people. There are many measures to alleviate this problem. First, as I discussed earlier, video cameras could be placed strategically in the jail, so it would document the majority of what goes on. The videos could then be reviewed by the public defender. Furthermore, for prison guards, I would institute a one strike and you are out policy as far as beatings. Legally, they can only get physical if they think they are in danger. Therefore if it is proven that they beat an inmate without the pre-condition, they get fired. All of these changes would be easy to institute, and must be made. We need to change and save the system, it is badly broken. For people to trust their government, their government must trust them.

Before we go to Iraq and other places to install democracies we should look at our own backyard for violations of human rights. Likewise before putting national attention on the human rights of would-be terrorists in Guantanimo, we need to focus on our own citizens and promote their human rights.

To accomplish these changes, the judicial system needs to be corrected. Our criminal law system is inherently not fair. If poor people commit a crime, they have to use the public defender to represent them. If a rich person commits a crime he can use a more qualified and better criminal defense attorney. If two people who are equal in every other respect, other than net worth, both murder their wives, the richer person has a better chance to be free because he has more money and can therefore afford a better attorney. Government attorneys should defend all criminal defendants, rich and poor. Imagine what the outcry would be in this country if rich people were forced to use public defenders and poor people got the best attorneys. When criminal law is the issue, we must think of the public's safety. Therefore, that should override the right of the rich to hire expensive attorneys. When it comes to crime the system needs to be equal for every single citizen. When it comes to prosecuting criminal cases, government attorneys do it. Imagine if victims of crime could hire expensive attorneys instead of government prosecutors to prosecute cases. As ridiculous as that sounds, the same happens for wealthy defendants. Another aspect of criminal cases that should be changed is that lie detector tests should be used, although they are not 100% effective, neither are juries. This would just be another factor for juries to think about in criminal cases it would not be dispositive.

In all cases our jury system should be changed. In the times of the framers of the Constitution everyone in their communities really were their peers. We should have a jury of two former judges or government attorneys and three laymen. That way the people with legal experience could explain the law to the others, and more informed decisions would be made. At the same time the laymen would still have voting power, because they would have an advantage of three to two. There are so many different kinds of people in our society that it is no longer a jury of our peers.

As was previously mentioned, in the health care section, juries give medical malpractice awards of tens of millions of dollars and often more than that. How does a jury of laymen know anything about medicine? For these cases at least one retired medical doctor should be added to the jury, again to educate the juries on medical matters. There is too much power given to inexperienced laymen in our judicial system. They decide who goes to jail and who doesn't and which doctors pay exorbitant amounts in malpractice punitive damages and which ones do not. These are just a few examples. The system must be overhauled for the ultimate benefit of everyone. Informed decisions are universally the best decisions.

Religion

I normally would not mention my personal feelings on religion, because that is my business. However, I am a pragmatic realist and I realize to succeed in American politics I must. I do not just believe in God, I know He exists. There is a difference between faith and certainty. I am certain. I have only prayed a handful of times for matters that I consider gravely important. Every single time I have prayed, God has answered. I do not need to go to a church or a temple with strangers and have someone preach to me to feel the Lord's presence. I feel the Lord's presence every single day of my life. That is all I have to say about my religion. I could not care less whether others believe or not. That is their business and certainly not mine. However, when the religion of others leads to hate and the death of innocent Americans, it becomes my business.

I respect all religions as long as they do not preach hate and violence against people who do not believe what they believe. Religion has no business in government, because religion is by its nature anti-democratic that is especially true in the intent the founding fathers had with the separation of church ands state. There is no religion that represents all Americans, but when religion influences government policy, it affects everyone, believers and non-believers alike. Imagine if atheists controlled the government and began implementing laws in religious private schools outlawing prayer. This would rightfully be completely unacceptable to certain religious people in this country. Our government policies must protect believers and non-believers and treat them equally. Our country has handled the religious debate badly. The atheists are usually just as much at fault as the religious. Both groups naturally treat each other with condescension. There should be mutual respect. Atheists are usually just as condescending as very religious people. They are always talking about science and how it is ridiculous to believe in God, just as the very religious are always talking about the bible and saying how ridiculous it is not to believe. The truth is that no one has definitive proof one way or the other, so, individuals should believe what they want and respectfully leave others alone. Have some respect.

I personally believe in God, although I do not think that he is an old man sitting on clouds. I also believe that He does not have time to worry about petty everyday things that happen in people's lives. The way I look at it if individuals do not know for sure if God exists or not, why not believe? For me it makes life more fulfilling to believe because it gives my existence more meaning, but it simply is not my business if others believe or not. In fact my father is an atheist and my mother does believe, but they have never tried to influence each other or me in that respect. If the world was the same way we would be much better. Philosophically, imagine how wrong it is to use violence to try to make others believe in God. That is what Christians did in the Middle Ages and what Muslim terrorists do now.

As far as people saying that science and evolution proves that God does not exist, I disagree. What if that was part of what God had in mind? Can we say with certainty that He didn't want humans and monkeys to evolve from a common predecessor? It can be said that everything in life, including science and evolution, was due to what He intended. The point is I do not know the details and neither do other people, but all we can do is respect others decision to believe or not believe. The problem with religion is that it deals in absolutes. For example, Jesus is God's son and that is just the way it is.

Another problem with religion is that scare tactics are used for absolutely no reason. Billy Graham was the most powerful preacher in this country before he died. Every single President would spend time with him. His daughter said recently that her generation and younger ones were the last ones that would ever exist because Israel was created in her lifetime and that the world was going to end any day now. She is a writer and somewhat of a preacher as well. The world ending part is complete and utter nonsense that is not based in reality, and saying those types of things will only have the effect of scaring people. In my view, religion should be used for hope, inspiration, and comfort, not to frighten people. Knowing the difference between right and wrong and never killing or hurting anyone in the name of religion is what matters. People can believe what they want, but they should never hurt others for not sharing their faith, nor attempt to force their beliefs on others. Jews are one religion that does not do that. You never see Jewish missionaries trying to get people to convert. I will always leave religion to the "experts" I am not here for that, I am here to accomplish the most I can in this world. I will worry about the next when I am there.

Regardless of how I feel the reality is that religion in our country has always had an intimate relationship with the political process. Candidates say they are religious and go to church, yet many act out in immoral ways. For example Bill Clinton, who held our highest elected position, was caught cheating on his wife. More recently another churchgoer, John Edwards, was caught cheating on his wife while she had cancer and he was running for the highest office. A Republican Senator was caught trying to have sex with another man in a bathroom. Some years ago, the governor of South Carolina, Mark Sanford, disappeared for a week to visit his Argentinian mistress. In all these cases, these men demonstrate moral hypocrisy. These politicians publicize that they go to church for show and to get the religious vote; it has nothing to do with their real lives. It is like saying that I am a vegetarian, so vegetarians will vote for me, when in reality I eat meat. The Christian Right is a group that seems to put a lot of faith in what candidates say, instead of what they do, regarding their religion. First, it is important to mention that I do not believe in most of the platform of the Christian Right. Specifically they are pro-life, anti-contraception, pro abstinence, anti stem-cell research, pro school prayer, anti-gay and anti-gay marriage. They have many more sophisticated views than that but these are really the only ones that I hear or care about at the moment.

As far as abortion, I understand both arguments. Pro-choice people think the mother has the right to abort the fetus. Pro-life people think that once inception has occurred the life force is sacred and should not be disturbed. Philosophically both of these views are valid. The reality is when very poor women have babies and they need welfare, the pro-life people are generally the ones who do not want taxes raised to support them and the ones who do not believe in redistribution of wealth. It is a bit hypocritical to fight for a life and then do nothing for it. Also, most people who are pro-life are for the death penalty. If God is the only one who gets to decide who lives and dies, regardless of the circumstances, how can someone be for the death penalty? But again, I respect the pro-life argument, but I disagree with it because I believe in self-determination on that issue, and I am for the death penalty. What I do respect about the religious is their passion. Albeit misdirected in certain cases, they are passionate people, and I am a very passionate person, so in the abstract I respect and relate to passion. And I know that when it is misdirected it can be a complete disaster (terrorists). But when I see passion I see the potential for great things as well as terrible things. I think it is necessary to respect the fundamental belief by some people that any life is life, even if that means at the point of conception. No one can disprove that scientifically. It is the concept I respect, not its application in our culture or the way the concept has been perverted by the far right and how that group has made abortion patients and abortion doctors the enemy in despicable ways. It should not be the law by any means, but it deserves my respect as a philosophical concept. Because abortion is legal now and the alternative is performing illegal abortions, where mother and baby frequently die, it makes more sense now to continue with pro-choice. What I do not understand is why there is so much animosity over the issue. There is clearly not one right or wrong answer. These are the types of disagreements that theoretically should be void of anger. It would be assumed that in an argument, when one side is really right and the other side is clearly wrong, that anger becomes present. For example, if a child molester has sex with ten-year-olds and takes the position that it is okay because it was consensual, he is completely wrong. If I had to argue the matter with him, I would probably get a bit angry. People need to save their anger and animosity for situations that demand them.

In the housing projects the ethnic groups with the highest proportion of teen pregnancies are Blacks and Hispanics. Many times this renders the mother and the kids dependent on society rather than contributors for the rest of their lives. We should give them more options. Give the mother a right to live well by advocating the use of condoms and the government offering free birth control for people in the housing projects. Although I do not think that condoms should be passed out in school, there should be a high school class that shows students how to put them on (obviously with a banana or a prosthetic penis). I know that many young people do not even know how to use them, and that is one of the reasons they skip it altogether. Abstinence obviously is not the answer. Any child that will be abstinent will be abstinent whether he learns it in school or not. A young person who decides he will not have sex until he gets married gets those values from home. Schools cannot even teach Math and English in inner city schools, so how can we expect them to teach a mature sophisticated concept like abstinence? Imagine telling a poor, young, black kid not to have sex, which to him is fun and free, because he should just abstain.

Other issues like no stem cell research and school prayer are very important to the Christian Right. I believe in stem cell research, because it is thought by the scientific community that stem cell research can lead to cures for disease. Whenever this is the case, the issue is not a question of "if" it is a question of "when". Our society cannot stop progress, but we can slow it down. I do not believe in governments that stop progress. The Christian Right is a group in the United States that is prone to stopping progress and unifying church and state.

School prayer in public schools is obviously wrong because every single American is not the same religion; we cannot favor one religion over another. If parents and members of the Christian Right are so intent on school prayer they have plenty of private school options for their children's education.

Although all the issues I have discussed are very important to our society, gay rights is the issue that gets the most media attention and the Christian Right is strictly at odds with the gay community. The Christian Right thinks homosexuals need to be converted to heterosexuality by "religious counseling" and they are completely against gay marriage under any circumstances. I believe in gay marriage for homosexuals. All this would mean in reality is that divorce attorneys would have more business; the more marriages that there are, the more divorce that there will be. Legalizing gay marriage would also have the effect of making the gay community happy. Many on the Christian Right would argue that marriage is sacred and that sanctity must be preserved. The reality is that marriage is not sacred at all in our society. We have politicians who have been married two, or three times and some more than that. We have people in our society who cheat on their wives and end up marrying the person they were cheating with. How sacred is that? Celebrities get married just to sell pictures of their weddings and for public relation stunts and then they subsequently get divorced months later. There are tons of examples of this behavior in the modern American society. The truth of the matter is that if homosexuals want to get married, it will not make any difference in anyone's life other than their own. If the Christian Right believes it is such a sin, then theoretically their God will deal with it when their day of judgment comes. We live in the here and now and I believe in self-determination on this issue as well.

I take the time to address homosexuals because the debate takes up too much time in the political arena. It is not that vital and the solution is just to give them what they want, they are not asking for that much. We live in a world and system that is totally not built for them, we live in a heterosexual world, and I do not think we need to make them feel further left out, they already feel left out as it is. I am not against homosexuals in the least; I believe anyone should do whatever they want in the privacy of their own bedrooms. I just do not need to hear about it ad nauseam. Whenever you are a minority that is different than the majority life will be rough. Just ask the Jews or members of the black community. Just like them, gays will never be like everyone else, because they are not like everyone else. One matter I do not understand when it comes to the gay community is that they feel that everyone should love them, it is not even okay to just be neutral towards them. The gays are just like everyone else, in the sense that there are good people and bad in the gay community. For some reason if you point out the bad in their group, you are a hateful person all of a sudden. But it is okay to point out the bad in any other group in this country, like Arabs or the black community for example. That is not right. We need to get past all of this as a society and spend more time discussing and solving issues that are much more vital for the world and to me personally, for example I care more about victims of genocide around the world than gay issues.

One issue that is consequential is homosexual adoption. I believe that in this case the mother of the child being adopted should have the right to decide if her child goes with a gay or straight couple. It is one thing for homosexuals to be able to have children, but a much more important matter is the welfare of the child. Like it or not any child that is raised by two homosexuals will go through a hell of a time growing up and being mocked. Whether this is right or wrong (and it is very wrong) is not the issue, it is a fact of life. The child's interests are the most important; therefore it seems right for his biological mother to make the decision.

Because of some positions like all the ones mentioned in this section, some Americans look at the Christian Right as a fringe group. In this country they are considered by many to be an extremist group. Members of the far left have compared them to Islamic terrorist groups. How many Christian groups from this country have ever gone to a foreign country and committed a terrorist act to promote pro-life or school prayer? None. Most people that are so rabidly anti-Christian are Christians themselves. They are upset because they feel that the other group is looking down at them and preaching. But that is what the first amendment is all about. It is strange that in the Muslim world, it is the radicals who are constantly complaining about the moderates. In the U.S. it seems that the left complains more about the Christian Right, than the other way around. I understand that it is sad that the Christian Right has so much power because they all vote, and they specifically have so much power in the Republican Party because they are loyal to it. They have about the same magnitude of voting power as the black community does to the Democrats.

Here, my idea of having more political parties in this country becomes relevant. The Christian Right should form their own political party separate from the Republican Party. That way they can elect their own representatives who represent their exact platform, not a Republican that represents a mish-mash of their platform along with the rest of the Republicans' ideas. This would seem, at first, like a loss to the Republicans, but then they could really move to the foundation of their policy, which is small government and low taxes, and focus on issues that are historically conservative. They could dedicate their time to many more important issues. In the meantime, Congressmen elected by the Christian Right Party could propose bills about matters that are crucial to them, but not really to the rest of the country. That is the basic idea of a democracy that represents hundreds of millions of people. Everyone's views, one way or another, need to be represented. A religious group that votes and stands for basically the opposite of the Christian Right are the Jews.

There are still many negative feelings towards Jews and Israel as a country. The reasons why are interesting and something people may not notice at first glance. Jews have historically been pacifists. Only after the European Nazis attempted to wipe them out of existence did they finally resort to using force to defend their very existence. From pogroms to terrorist attacks, they have been the target of hate, envy and genocide for the past two thousand years. Ever since Judah supposedly turned Jesus in to the Romans; blame has wrongfully been focused on the Jews. If that story is indeed true, why do people blame the Jews, who told the Romans where Jesus was, instead of the Romans who actually murdered him? Now we find ourselves in the twenty first century and widespread anti-Semitism is as vicious as ever.

No minority has been despised with the same vitriol as the Jews. For example, there may be prejudice aimed at Mexicans or Blacks in this country, but the hate is not so outrageous that people are blaming the blacks for September 11th. Some did blame the Jews for the attacks, saying that Israel carried out the attacks and it was their plan. Israel is the country that proportionally fights terrorism the most and they are blamed by some for the biggest terrorist attack in history. The reason that Jews are hated so much is that they are the only minority in the world that economically outperforms the majority. No one can really come up for a reason why the Jews, as a whole, consistently outperform. So, people make up lies and stereotypes. For example, they say Jews are cheap and dishonest when it comes to business, opposed to everyone else that is theoretically so generous and honest when it comes to business matters.

One reason Jews outperform is because they have been systematically bred throughout the years to have a population of survivors of superior beings (within their own group). Envy of someone who has more money, for no obvious reason is the impetus for hate. The worst is that people cannot understand why they are doing so well. The reason is very easy and scientific. Natural selection is a theory of evolution that states that the fittest survive and the weak die. Millions of Jews have been being killed for the last hundreds of years. Thousands were killed in the Spanish Inquisition in the 1500s and obviously millions were killed in the Holocaust. What this means is that the survivors had to have some type of intelligence, or strength, or something that the others did not to withstand the onslaughts and survive. Some had fake passports and managed to evade the Nazis. That requires intelligence, courage and passion. These survivors then reproduce with other survivors to create a race of people that are the best of the best of the Jews.

A useful analogy and phenomenon is the insect repellant situation. Every time an insect repellant is used to protect crops a very small number of the insects survive because they have a mutant genetic makeup that resists the repellant. These survivors reproduce and a new updated mutant specific repellant has to be made. Then the cycle continues. The point is every new generation is stronger than the last. Christians have never been slaughtered as a whole on the same scale as Jews and neither have Muslims. Therefore, the weak and idiotic Christians and Muslims have reproduced with basically the same chance of survival as the intelligent and strong Christians and Muslims. Therefore, by definition there will be a much higher proportion of unsuccessful Christians and Muslims than Jews. This is basic logic. The Jews are hated because of circumstances the majority of the people at the time, Christian Spaniards during the inquisition, and German Nazis (most of which were Christians whether they practiced or not) caused. This is absolutely absurd, sick, disgusting and unacceptable. It is like shooting one of your employees in the leg and then hating him because he walks with a limp. Pogroms, the Inquisition, and Nazis forced the strongest of the strong of the Jews to survive under unbelievable conditions and now people hate them because they have such strong qualities that are based on the qualities that they needed to survive.

I care deeply about this issue because, as I have stated, my grandfather almost lost his life due to hateful prejudice in the Holocaust and his brothers lost theirs. My father's aunt lost her children and the Nazis massacred her while she was pregnant. This has led me to be completely intolerant of unfounded and arbitrary prejudice of any kind. Anti-Semitism plagues the world now, as always. There are college professors in this country who deny that the Holocaust ever happened. This is completely unacceptable. Imagine if there was a white college professor who stated that slavery did not happen and it was all an invention of the black community to make people feel sorry for them. Obviously, that would be unacceptable and that professor would not be teaching anywhere in the United States. So why should the situation with the Jews be any different? It is because they are being punished for being successful. In this country, as in many places, it is a commonly accepted premise that it is okay to persecute people who are successful. Under this thought process economic success is something that should be denigrated and not celebrated.

The reason this phenomenon occurs is because people will believe anything if it is against the Jews. Whenever a minority does better financially than the majority, there will be this type of hatred. Furthermore, all the other minorities will be jealous of the one minority that is beating the majority. The majority of the people and the other minorities cannot admit to themselves that they are less capable, not as hard working, or whatever else so they have to make up lies and punish the most successful minority: Jews. This is human nature at its worst. What is truly fascinating is that one reason the Jews do so much better proportionately is because of the hate others have towards them. Regardless, American Jews as a whole still try to help others politically as much as possible. The Jews are the only group of Americans that vote against their economic interests.

Every group of Americans vote according to what makes more sense to them economically (there are exceptions but here we are discussing the majority of each group). For instance, the majority of the black community are not wealthy, therefore, they vote for Democrats who vow to raise taxes on the rich and give the middle class and the poor more benefits. The majority of millionaires vote for Republicans, because they promise to keep taxes low. The majority of Jews vote for Democrats, although raising taxes does not favor them because they are usually wealthy. Obviously there are exceptions, but this is the overwhelming majority. It is ironic that the way Jews vote goes against the stereotype that they are cheap. If they were truly cheap they would be Republicans, because Republicans have historically had fiscal policy that is more favorable to the wealthy. The reason they vote Democratic is because Jews have been underdogs and gone through hard times, therefore they choose the party that they think will help people who are struggling and they relate to these people, setting their own economic interests aside in the process.

The Jews have been fighting for their life since they have existed. To this day they continue to fight in the Middle East. The reason they seem to succeed in the face of growing adversity is because of a very strong gene pool and the very people that tried to destroy them made them stronger. When certain people do not want to accept this fact, they turn to other ways of satisfying their anti-Semitic addiction. Some say the Holocaust did not occur, others say that all the problems in the Middle East are the fault of Israel, and most become anti-Israel as a replacement for anti-Semitism. This is convenient because being anti-Israel is very en vogue internationally.

Imagine a Middle East where the entire territory-Iraq, Iran, Jordan, Egypt, Syria, Turkey, Kuwait, Saudi Arabia-was populated and controlled by Jewish kings and dictators who constantly murdered their own people. Now try to fathom that the Muslims only had control of a small strip of land (which is now Israel). Furthermore, imagine that in that small strip of land there existed a hostile Jewish population that thought that they had the right to the land. Those Jews use terrorism and the killing of civilians to try to reach their goals, and in response the Muslims go into the territories to wipe out the terrorism. Do you think that world opinion would be on the Jewish side, as in reality where the reverse exact situation is true and European opinion is on the Palestinian side? Being anti-Israeli is the new acceptable form of anti-Semitism.

The Media, Politics, and Society

The media in the United States is broken and it has failed our citizens. There is a major difference between reporting real issues that are happening in the country and the world and sensationalizing whatever will get networks more ratings. There is so much commentating now that it is rare to get an objective view about anything. It is no longer news, it is entertainment from the 24/7 cable news networks. An example of unfair sensationalizing news coverage is how the media gives much more attention to a white child disappearing compared to when a black child disappears. Continuing on this theme, when there is black on white crime, it gets much more coverage than black on black crime. Also, when there is Israeli on Arab killing, that is given a hundred more times attention than Arab on Arab killing. When Israelis killed about 10 people defending themselves in the Turkish flotilla situation that got more attention than an Arab leader slaughtering over 100 of his own people who were peacefully demonstrating for human rights and freedom. In Syria children are being murdered everyday protesting for those rights now. If Israel did what the Syrians are doing for just one week to the Palestinians, the entire world press would be covering it and criticizing Israel ad nauseam, as they did in Israel's week long conflict with Hamas in 2012. Why should that get more coverage? Are Palestinian lives worth more than Syrian lives? If so who makes that decision?

Most of the people who watch the media in the United States are white, a fact based on demographics, so the media plays to their audience for ratings and money. That is okay if someone has a TV show, but these people say it is the news. It is not the real news. It is the news for a certain group of target audience Americans. The government lets the media tell them what issues are of perceived importance and they act on that. The media should be about the truth and informing the public on what is really happening in this country and the world, not just picking and choosing certain stories because they will give them the highest ratings. It is a disgrace and the American media is completely lost. It is sad to know how the U.S. has fallen from what it used to be. Walter Cronkite, for example, reported the news in a dignified manner. However, it can be fixed.

Media focus needs to be put on the things that really matter in the world, like whenever genocide takes place, the world needs to cover it intensely. Putting attention on issues like that forces citizens to pay attention, and that matters, helps and can lead to change. The way the media is now, if some politician is caught cheating on his wife or he is caught taking part in lewd sexual behavior, the media becomes obsessed with it while they more or less ignore things that matter much more to our country and to the world. In other countries, world news is the focus on a daily basis and they are better informed than Americans. Taxi cab drivers in other countries know more about what is happening in the world than many

Congressmen in this country. But the problem with politicians does not stop at them being incredibly uninformed, they operate in a complete culture of lies.

As far as politicians and the media are concerned, so much time and money could be saved if everyone just stopped with the pandering and nonsense and was honest. If that were the case, our society could move with lightning speed; it is that easy. When the media and politicians lie, they know what they are doing and it is all some sick game that society has gotten very used to playing. Honesty on a mass scale would have a very strong impact on the everyday lives of our citizens. We have a system designed for leaders and politicians to lie just to qualify and be able to survive at their jobs. It is a prerequisite. When candidates run for office they have to say they are for everything (the entire platform) that whichever party they are running for believes, whether they truly believe these things or not. For example, a Republican running for office must say he is pro-life, and a Democrat running for office must say he is pro-choice, whether they truly believe in that or not. That issue has very little to do with the other beliefs each party has, but regardless, the candidates are locked into these beliefs they may or may not have. Most professions are not like that and honesty is valued very much. Doctors, for example, are one profession where individuals cannot lie because lives and careers depend on it. They have to absolutely tell the truth. See the contrast? They are trained to be honest. Why can't everything be that way? Honesty is precious and fragile and we must fight to protect it. Even if opinions differ, as long as both parties are being honest with their views and feelings, there is dignity in that.

Most of the media is all about criticizing the person or political party that they do not support, instead of talking about constructive ideas and solutions to the country's problems, or talking about the positives of a candidate or party. I do not even understand negative campaign ads. I know why they use them to attempt to make the opponent look weak, but wouldn't real leaders with confidence use paid airtime to discuss their own accomplishments and ideas? Politicians should concern themselves with the opponents and take them on in debates; that is why debates exist.

Another matter I do not fully understand is why so much attention is given to how actors feel about politics. What happens with a lot of actors, who involve themselves in politics, is that their own lives are so fake and unreal, because they are always playing other characters leading other people's lives in a fantasy world, and that creates an emptiness inside them. They have such a craving to be real because they are paid to be artificial. This manifests itself in people like Angelina Jolie attempting to "save the world", and Sean Penn going to controversial places to try to be real and get the attention all actors crave. It is still all fake and he will never get that reality he is looking for, because when you go to controversial places they treat you in a different way because you are an actor and you are famous. It is not real. If he were any other

American they would probably arrest him for being a spy, if they did that then he would get some genuine reality. Other famous people, who are not actors, like to get involved in politics as well. People like Warren Buffet and other billionaires say Americans should pay more taxes to the federal government. I do not understand why they just do not do it, no one is stopping them, but do not tell other people what they have to do. As far as abortion, Democrats are pro-choice, because they follow the principle that citizens should be free to do what they want and should not tell others what they have to do. It is the same stance many have on gay marriage. So do not be hypocrites and let people do what they want with their own money. If people want to pay more taxes they can do it, but again do not tell others what they should do.

Celebrities are much richer than almost everyone in our society and they live in homes with 20 bathrooms. They specialize in burning money on things that do not matter, and the world they live in is fake and alien to the average American. Most of those celebrities know very little about politics, but that does not stop them from telling others who they should vote for. When they start talking politics, I think it would be better for everyone if they just stuck to acting. Something that would help is if celebrities used all the money raised for politicians to buy U.S. Treasury Bonds instead.

Politicians in this country always have to find an enemy to blame: first it was Bush, then Palin briefly, and now it's the Tea Party for the Democrats and it is Obama or whoever the sitting President is (if he is a Democrat) for the Republicans. It is always someone else's fault. How about giving the public detailed plans regarding how to fix things and coming up with new useful ideas instead of constantly laying blame on someone, anyone, and always finger pointing. These two parties would rather disagree with animosity than come together for the country. Even when the country is having real problems at a faster rate than it ever has. Who cares whose fault a problem is? Just fix it. If a sick patient goes to a doctor, does the doctor start talking about whose fault it is, or does he treat the patient and solve the problem? What does that say about politicians? The reason this is so hard for many of our citizens to accept is because they have been injected with propaganda since the day they were born. There is absolutely nothing wrong with debating different political philosophies but let's have some mutual respect for the opponents. Let's be gentlemen. The money corrupted the political process a long time ago, the system just got citizens to believe in the fallacy that it was one side's fault over the other. Should a country as complex as ours only have two sides and two groups of the population that go crazy over one side against the other?

It is all nonsense and the public are the pawns. 90% of the people in Congress, on both sides, are wealthy and corrupt and they only care about keeping their cushy jobs and "power". They do not care about you. If Congress did care about the people, there would be more former military in Congress, citizens that have tangibly sacrificed for this country, instead of people who only know how to fundraise from other people who think they have the answers. Our Congress should also be made up of accountants, physicians, teachers, doctors, engineers, computer programmers, economists, scientists, former FBI, CIA etc. Start using your voting power to get real people in and say no to the typical Washington politician lawyer that has only showed that he has the ability to make money. The type of people I mentioned are used to doing real things and not just raising money. The idea of the United States and a totally corrupt free democracy and country has been perverted. We can still save it.

Energy

Gas prices are increasing very quickly and we have reached a crisis level. This is due to the high prices of oil that are spiraling out of control. There are certain things that make the price of oil go up and others that make the price of oil go down. These include supply, demand, and speculation.

When oil supply goes up, if demand stays the same, prices go down. When demand goes up, if supply stays the same, prices go up. If demand goes down, if supply stays the same, prices go down. So, if we combine the best scenarios for prices to go down, we must increase supply and decrease demand. We can absolutely increase supply by many methods like off shore drilling, which means oil drilling off the coast into the Pacific Ocean, or doing the same in the Atlantic Ocean. Experts have stated that there is oil there. We can also increase supply by drilling in the Arctic National Wildlife Refuge (ANWR, Alaska) and many other locations in the United States where experts know there is oil. There are 20,000 miles in ANWR, where there is oil, in an arctic forest preserve. Surely, the environmentalists will not hijack the financial interests of the American public for this relatively small amount of real estate. We must drill everywhere we possibly can in the United States.

Opponents of drilling have been saying, ironically for the past ten years, that we should not drill because we would not see the benefits for another ten years. This is the losing mentality, shortsighted, type thinking that should be eradicated. If there is a ten-year process that we can take part in that would make us more self-sufficient in oil and give U.S. citizens an affordable option to fill up our gas tanks, we can wait ten years. What is the alternative? Are we all going to ride bikes to work? Some politicians say that the only thing we can do is lower demand. The reason that this alone would not work is that a big part of the reason oil prices have increased is that demand has skyrocketed. India and China have huge populations. For many years neither country had much of a middle class, and therefore many people could not afford cars. Now India and China are big players in the global economy. They are forming middle classes that can begin to afford "luxury" items like cars. So now there are more people (millions more) that want oil for their cars. If the supply stays the same in these situations, prices go up. So, it is a given that global demand is up. Nothing we can do will stop that, however we can lower our own demand. This alone is not the solution; this must be done in concert with raising the supply (as outlined above). The way to lower demand is by researching alternative sources of fuel. We have groundbreaking research in the areas of solar energy, wind energy, nuclear energy, and the use of batteries in cars. Hybrid cars are also selling well. The government must make hybrids attractive to every car buyer. Many state governments are offering rebate checks; something of this nature must be done on the federal level. The federal government must invest heartily in these programs. Not simply give these companies money to develop better ways to get better fuels, but actually invest dollars in their companies.

Another measure that must be taken is that ethanol, as fuel, should be abandoned. It is a scam. It takes a lot of corn to make a little bit of usable fuel and in the meantime the price of corn skyrockets. This is a case of less supply and same demand, and thus the price goes up. The price of corn has risen dramatically in the past years. This makes food more expensive. Opponents of these common sense measures to tackling the energy crisis like to blame speculators.

Speculators are investors that think that oil is going to go up in the future. Because of what they think, they buy the oil stock for futures, the United States Oil fund, stock symbol "USO", for example. The stock tracks what oil does every day. So imagine buying that oil stock and three months later it is up 20%. At this point the stock is sold and the owner makes a nice profit. The buyer may hold on to it longer and make more money, or hold on to it and lose money if it goes down. People attack the speculators because they state that speculators are artificially making the price of oil go up. The thought process is that if a million people buy a bunch of corn, or oil, or whatever, the price of that commodity will go up. However, for every buyer of USO there is a seller, so any attempt to regulate this would be ridiculous. Congress does not understand the basics of stocks and investing, therefore they should stay out of regulating it at this level. By buying a lot of something there is less supply. Again less supply same demand and the prices go up. I personally think it is very lame to blame the speculators, who are American investors who are trying to make an honest buck out of this situation. If speculators do have such a big effect, and the oil commodity truly acts like a stock, just start drilling and that would make the price go down. Regardless of when we would see the fruits of it, a stock's price reflects future activity and losses (more supply, lower price). So it is a win-win proposition.

If there is someone to blame for the oil crisis it is the Saudis. 15 of the 19 hijackers on 9/11 were from Saudi Arabia and that country cannot do us the favor of increasing supply? When I say increase, I do not mean a drop in the bucket either. I am talking about doubling the supply to the United States. We indirectly feed everyone in that country. We buy their oil more than anyone else. President George W. Bush went there asking for more oil in the middle of our crisis, during his second term, and they had the gall to turn him down. A country that had 15 of its citizens crash into our buildings should be very ashamed of themselves and this should be the least that they can do for us.

Part Two

FOREIGN POLICY

SECURITY

DEFENSE

Cuba

Ever since Fidel Castro rose to power in Cuba, the United States has had an embargo there. What this means is that we do not trade with Cuba. The consequences to Cuba's economy are devastating. The main reason the U.S. started the embargo was because Cuba was a communist country and communists were our enemy and our primary threat. This is no longer the case. Communism is no longer a threat to our national security. Now certain people have said that the reason we continue the embargo is because Cuba does not give its people human rights and basic freedoms. Our most important trade partner, China, is the biggest and most powerful communist country in the world. Also, like Cuba, China does not extend full human rights or freedom to its citizens. So if the rationale for the embargo against Cuba is that they are communists and they do not give human rights to their people, how is it not hypocritical to trade with China, which is exactly like Cuba as far as those things go? We can no longer have inconsistent foreign policy; our foreign policy must be uniform. Although Fidel Castro and his brother Raul, who is now the leader of Cuba, are responsible for the deaths of thousands of innocent Cubans, the United States must lift the trade ban on Cuba. It is not the fault of the Cuban people that they are led by an oppressive regime. If the embargo is lifted, it will ultimately help the people, but it will not really make a difference to Fidel Castro, who is not even their leader anymore. He is living under great personal conditions anyway. We do not even have a total embargo against the worst country in the world, Iran. Can anyone honestly say that Iran is not more oppressive and anti-American than Cuba? I do not remember Cuba ever taking American hostages or funding terrorist groups and housing Al-Qaeda, or building a nuclear weapon to destabilize the Middle East and wipe out our ally Israel. Iran has done all these things.

The whole point of the Radical Party is to develop and implement the right solutions, with a complete disregard to special interest groups that are undermining the right thing to do. I am referring to the Cubans in Miami who are so, albeit justifiably, angry that they do not want the embargo lifted while Castro or his brother is still in power. Once the embargo is lifted American Cubans have every right not to buy any Cuban goods. However, they should not have the right to tell another American whether he can or cannot buy a Cuban cigar, especially if the sale of that Cuban cigar would help poor people in Cuba. The cigar trade alone would boost Cuba's economy and help put food in the mouths of poor Cubans who are right off the coast of Florida. When Cuba does become a democratic country, after the death of Fidel Castro and Raul Castro, I am sure the Cuban people will be appreciative that we lifted the embargo sooner rather than later.

China

What is happening now in China is not communism, it is more like an aggressively capitalistic middle of the road (relatively speaking) police state. They may still talk about communism and hang on to some inconsequential ideals of it, but it is not communism. China finally understood that what matters in government, at the end of the day, is the bottom line economically. Human rights and civil liberties are the other things that matter in a civilized society and both will get to China one way or another. I predict their government will do that on their own, the other option, which is a revolution when the growing middle class gets sick and tired of the oppression, would completely destabilize their economy. Do not think that they are as powerful as perception paints them to be. They are one revolution away from that economy being in chaos for a while. China is not progress and the future. The free people of the world and the Chinese people that want freedom are progress and the future.

Because China is an economic superpower, it is my opinion that they have different responsibilities than they did before. If a country is making a large amount of money from the world, it has a direct responsibility to be positively involved in world affairs and threats, like Iran. The analogy would be that if an owner of a business is successful, he has a responsibility to his customers. Isn't it about time that China has a statesman that does big things, that aren't just economic? Every great country has people like them and China does not. Diplomacy is huge, and judging from their behavior as a nation, they only use it to make money. And China has the gall to call itself a communist country? Aren't the communists the ones that theoretically care about other things way ahead of money? If China truly gave up all their communist ideals in the pursuit of money, then they should give their people human rights and freedom as well. Or do one thing that will help the world, make a real diplomatic appeal to get Iran to abandon its nuclear weapons program. Or at least do not get in the way when the world is trying to help people that are getting massacred when no one else will help.

Recently the UN was going to pass a resolution to punish Syria for the atrocities their government is committing to the people there and China and Russia blocked it. China should realize the world does not trust it. While countries do business with them, in reality, there is not much trust. Do something to earn it with Iran. I wonder how the country will handle its first real foreign policy test, when the entire world is watching. All signs point to failure and no one will remember how great the olympic opening ceremonies were, in the long run, if the country gets this one wrong. If China cared half as much about the Iran situation, as they did about the olympics, specifically to show the world how great it was, this matter would probably be resolved.

China could have a big role in making Iran abandon its nuclear program peacefully. I know they never make a foreign policy move that does not directly benefit them economically, whether it is good for the world or not. So I will explain it in a way China should understand. If China does nothing about Iran, Israel or the U.S. or both will blow Iran to Kingdom Come, and as a consequence oil prices will go absolutely through the roof. Iran might respond by blowing up oil fields and interfering with the Straights of Hormuz, even if they do not take those measures the oil situation in Iran will be a mess. It will cause economic chaos in China for years. I guarantee that if it is not addressed, the military option will be used. It is no longer a question of if, it is a question of when and time is ticking. China may be naive enough to question America's resolve, but surely they are not stupid enough to question Israel's.

North Korea

Kim Jong Il, the dictator of North Korea died recently. His young son took over control of that country. We should immediately invite Kim Jong Il's son to the U.S. He is 27 or 28 and that is a very impressionable age. Give him a tour of the U.S. to the best spots and show him how the most modern country in the entire world lives. Kim Jung Un (the son) loves American movies, NBA basketball, and Michael Jordan is his idol. Take him to NBA games, he could meet the players, and spend time with them. What 28 year-old basketball fanatic would turn that down? Also, introduce him to Hollywood people and he can spend time with actors and actresses. Again what 28 year old who loves basketball and movies would not love that? That is just the tip of the iceberg of what we could do with him if he came for a month. Then tell him to hold democratic elections in his country and give up the nuclear weapon programs he has. Offer him some land here and show him what life is like in the U.S. That is diplomacy.

North Korea and South Korea should merge in the future and this could be a huge first step. Once they do merge, a united Korean economy would be very robust. South Korea's economy is already doing very well and they would be able to absorb people (the North Koreans) who are literally hungry to come work whatever jobs they can. South Korea would also absorb North

Korea's military, which is stronger than South Korea's. North Koreans get jobs, regular lives, and freedom and South Korea gets a very strong military. Currently the U.S. military has about 30,000 troops in South Korea and they are there to protect South Korea (weaker military) from North Korea (stronger military). If they merged we would be able to leave and that would save us tons of money. This is a win-win-win situation. Everyone wins and that is rare in foreign policy. Wealthy South Koreans, there are many, could invest and develop North Korea. Diplomacy has really deteriorated in the past years in the U.S.

Diplomacy is an art form and its most important function is to stop wars by talking and making deals. It is about time the new generation takes over some aspects of it when foreign policy comes to dealing with young leaders. Someone with poor social skills who has led a boring life and who works at the State Department is not going to get it done. The State Department needs to be revolutionized. They need to have a wide range of employees from different backgrounds, different skill sets, and from a wide range of age groups. I would have someone for every conceivable situation. It may be impossible to deal with certain countries diplomatically, like Iran, but it is necessary to try as best as can be before defining it as a failure. The alternative, war or military intervention, should always be an option, but it should always be the last option. Talk, talk, talk until no one can talk anymore and then explore other options.

Terrorism

To discuss terrorism, it is first necessary to define it. For some reason Americans have been scared to do this. Terrorists are people who target and kill innocent civilians to advance political goals. Distorted people like some of the far left Americans and Islamists call the U.S. and Israel terrorists. This is ironic because the U.S. and Israel do everything they can to avoid damage to civilians when they attack, as opposed to terrorists who do everything they can to damage civilians when they attack.

After 9/11 more options should have been discussed in regards to the war against terror. When a cataclysmic event, such as those attacks, happens on American soil, everything is on the table. At the time no one was offering a more cogent plan than the one the government had in place. Their actions, in invading Afghanistan and Iraq, are certainly better than any of the alternatives that were being discussed. However, one problem is that the extreme option was not being discussed. We knew who and where the culprits of the attack were and it was time to at least discuss historic action. This action was not simply attacking Afghanistan while Bin Laden and most of the key members of Al-Qaeda escaped. If our intelligence determined that the Taliban knew the whereabouts of Bin Laden, we should have told the Taliban that if they did not deliver Bin Laden and the rest of Al-Qaeda, within a reasonable amount of time, that we would drop a nuclear bomb on Kabul. Just because we would make such a threat does not mean we would have to go through with it if they did not deliver Bin Laden in the relevant amount of time. With foreign policy, there is nothing wrong with bluffing or using creative ploys to try to achieve certain goals with the least amount of resistance.

It is important to note that if that were the immediate route we would have taken, that we would have either had Bin Laden or we would have dropped a nuclear bomb. Both of these options are better than what happened. Why should we care to rebuild Afghanistan and help them? Why should American troops die in Afghanistan to make their country better? Why should doctors, who could not afford the ridiculous cost of medical school in this country, have to go to the armed forces to pay for their medical education in exchange for service in Afghanistan? We should have given the Afghanis a one-month ultimatum to make the decision. Imagine destroying the enemy and reaching our immediate strategic goal and not losing one American soldier. This should always be our military philosophy: destroying the enemy with the least amount of domestic casualties. The nuclear option enables us to accomplish our goals quickly and efficiently and more importantly no American families, who have relatives in the armed forces, have to suffer completely unnecessary loss of life. Again, I am making the point that this should have been discussed as an option, it has its positives as well as its negatives. But I would try to see what the national mood of the people was concerning taking such action. It should have been part of the conversation.

Nationally, here in the U.S., there are many steps that we can employ to take the war on terror to the next level. A universal thumb print method of identification should be instituted; every American would have his thumbprint on record. This thumbprint would be first used in airports, then trains, and everywhere else a terrorist attack would be possible. Every foreigner entering our country would also have to be registered with the thumb print program, at his or her own expense of course. This way we would have records of who is where at all times and it would be virtually impossible for someone on the terror watch list to enter a high risk area without being immediately accosted. This would also prevent passport forgeries and things of that nature.

The next step would be to address the calamitous border situation with Mexico. Many terrorists could easily enter the U.S. via the border with Mexico. For example, a terrorist could easily enter the U.S. through Mexico, arm himself with explosives and blow himself up in a shopping center, bar, movie theatre, or any public place killing dozens of people. Therefore, we must secure the border with Mexico (after granting full amnesty to illegal immigrants as was discussed earlier). A positive side effect would be that illegal immigrants would be kept out of the U.S. Although the illegal immigrants take jobs that supposedly no one else wants in this country, this is no justification to turn a blind eye to the practice of illegal immigration. Many criminals enter the country and furthermore the immigrants that are doing jobs that no one else wants do not pay taxes. That means that they are making money off our country and paying nothing in return. They are essentially getting free education and healthcare because they pay no income taxes. They have an unfair advantage over our poor citizens and people from all over the world who would gladly do the jobs that they claim no one else would do. For example, millions of Africans who are currently the victims of genocide would love to come here and pick fruit. The solution is to first take an estimate of how many illegal aliens come across the border every day. Next give green cards to 50% of this amount in a legal fashion. This would allow us to keep tabs on Mexican immigrants making sure that no criminals are allowed in the country. Furthermore, if it were easier to get green cards less people would illegally try to get in the country. Also, if they were here legally they could continue doing the jobs no one else wants but the government could tax the money and generate more revenue. Allowing 50% of immigrants in this country would be a fine compromise for the Mexican American population who think there is nothing wrong with illegal aliens coming in from Mexico. The next question would be how to secure the borders.

I would propose using new tax money, from programs outlined in the social policy section of this book, to fund building an enormous electrical wire fence that runs across areas of heavy volume border crossing. They would be like fences used in prisons, however the electrical fences would not be designed to kill people that touch them they would be designed to provide a shock that puts people in a state similar to what a tazer gun does. A tazer gun makes people temporarily unconscious. Every time a person would be shocked this would trigger an alarm to the nearest border patrol to come arrest the illegal alien. This provides tangible consequences to illegal behavior. Philosophically what happens when there is no tangible punishment to illegal behavior is that people that take part in the illegal behavior stop thinking that there is anything wrong with the behavior. Furthermore, the perpetrators begin acting like the illegal action (crossing the border with no documentation) is a right. This is particularly grotesque. At this point, theoretically at least, the borders would be secure and the high-risk terrorist demographic would be out of this country. Therefore, as far as our borders, the homeland would be secure. Many people say that fences do not work, but this is just wrong. The Israelis have put fences to separate them from Palestinian territories to stop terrorists from coming into Israel and it works.

Israel's continued existence is due to the fact that they have demoralized and destroyed their enemies every time they have fought wars started by their opponents. They have done this while being grossly outmanned and outgunned. The point is that Arab countries understand the situation when they are hit hard. Most Arab armies are not strong and cannot succeed in traditional forms of warfare. They use their militaries to control and kill their own people. They have demonstrated that they always lose when they fight non-Arab opponents; therefore radicals in the Arab population have to resort to terrorism to attempt to advance their political goals. Therefore, to address the problem, terrorist groups need to be wiped out completely.

To wipe out the terrorists we would need to execute the international war on terror. Instead of occupying countries that may have terrorists, we should have dismantled terrorist training camps we know exist in Lebanon, Syria and Iran. We must give those countries ultimatums to either dismantle their terrorist camps, within a certain logical time frame, or suffer the consequences. The consequences would be that we would send our air force to destroy their terrorist camps in a surgical way. We would be in and out with minimal loss of American life. We will not stay in those countries or occupy them, just take out the terrorists. By destroying terrorist training camps, this initial plan of action gives tangible punishment to foreign countries that help terrorists, while we suffer minimal, if any, domestic loss of life. The age of terrorism requires this aggressive brand of foreign policy. The type of system outlined above would continue until we eradicated every terrorist training camp our intelligence knew about.

The reason that this may seem politically difficult is that many would interpret this move as the U.S. helping Israel because, some of the terrorist training camps would be for terrorists that primarily attack Israel. However, in many cases the terrorist groups would also be our major enemy. For instance the terrorist group Hezbollah who operates out of Lebanon is commonly seen as Israel's enemy. But, in the 1980s they drove a truck full of explosives into a U.S. marine barracks killing over 200 American soldiers. We still have not gotten our revenge. Completely dismantling Hezbollah would help Israel and us. Although there is nothing wrong with helping Israel, because they are one of our only true allies, this would not be our primary reason for the attacks. It is essential to realize that we can no longer make distinctions between terrorists that target Israel and those that primarily target other countries. Terrorism is terrorism and the philosophy and the manpower associated with terrorism must be eradicated. Imagine if McDonald's started serving poisoned food in every single one of its restaurants. It would be most important to shut down all of the McDonald's restaurants in the U.S. first, but it would also be crucial to shut down every chain in the world, that would be the only way to remove all the poisoned food and protect the entire world, not just us. If we are to fight terrorism, we must fight all terrorism. This is the only way to shut down the cancer that terrorism is. At this point the homeland would be secured and the terrorists we know about in Syria, Lebanon, and Iran would be wiped out. This would be a very healthy start to the operation. Now would be the time to eradicate the philosophy that promulgates terror. This is currently being done by the U.S. spending funds it doesn't have on public relations campaigns to win over the Muslim people in the Middle East. This strategy is nonsense.

Although the steps of securing the homeland and wiping out known terrorist camps were not done, Iraq was the best option on the table to start fighting terrorism. There would have been fewer terrorists in the insurgency if we would have taken the initial steps that I outlined. But regardless, the American people need to know the real reason why the war is justifiable in the final analysis. The end does justify the means. Iraq was the most powerful secular country that had vast oil fields in the area and relative to the other Arab countries they were relatively progressive with women's rights. This made them ripe for a democracy. The point of going to Iraq was that if we created a successful democracy that could fund itself, primarily with oil sales, it would serve as a model for the region. I do not think that it is just a coincidence that quickly after we freed Iraq that Yemen, Egypt, Libya, and Syria began movements for democracy in a region that never had it before. Of course Iraq was an influence, so it already has served its function as a model for the region. People in democracies can stop blaming others for their problems and realize hard work leads to an opportunity for a happy life. Terrorists are basically people that have given up on life. They have gotten to a point where they feel that life affords them no option. If a man has an opportunity for a good job, a wife and a family he will more than likely not become a terrorist.

Moderate Muslims claim they are the majority and get blamed for terrorist acts of only a few. If they truly are the majority why don't they take control of the terrorist problem in their countries and handle it themselves?

If 1% of Americans were causing major world problems all over the planet, trust me, the U.S. would handle it. We wouldn't just constantly say how we have mostly good guys and that the bad elements are giving us a bad name, like many Middle Eastern countries do, we would do something about it. It is time for all Muslims to choose, whether they are with us or against us. In this fight, there are no Switzerlands. If Middle Eastern countries are with us, they must give up all terrorists who operate in their countries. Whether these countries like us is completely irrelevant.

Pouring millions of dollars into ridiculous programs that are geared towards "making them like and understand us" is a complete waste of time. All the Americans that ponder things like, "I just don't know why they don't like us" do not get it and they never will. The Americans that say things like, "If I were them I would hate the U.S. as well" are a waste of space. If they really feel that way why don't they donate the majority of their money to aid poverty in the Middle East? The premise that we need to waste money on programs to make the Muslims in the Middle East like us more is absurd. Americans sound like some insecure junior-high girl, who is not popular, wondering why people do not like her. I am of the school of thought that when someone has problems with others always assume that they are the ones that must change. If a person has any self-confidence or self-respect he will always start this type of analysis with that mind set. It does not mean that you are always faultless, but at least have enough confidence in yourself to start the analysis in the fashion that is most promising to you. Imagine owning a store and having one particular customer that is loyal and keeps the owner in business by buying the product. Would it make sense to kill that customer? In the previous analogy America is that customer and the Middle East is the owner of the business. Americans buy the most oil from that region. If we stopped buying oil from that region tomorrow, they would have a catastrophic economic crisis. That would really be unleashing the gates of hell (as Arabs and Iranians always threaten). They treat us, their best customers, as the enemy.

Terrorists from the region want to kill Americans, the people that put food on the table of Muslims throughout the Middle East. This is completely illogical from a business standpoint. Do businessmen hate their customers? Do lawyers hate their clients? Do doctors hate their patients? Of course they do not. The majority of the people in the Middle East hate Americans, because they are delusional. We are dealing with psychopaths who are working as hard as they can to destroy our very way of life. So we are supposed to understand why the radicals hate us? For that you need psychiatrists, not diplomats. They are so overwhelmed with envy and hatred that they are completely psychotic. If there is a schizophrenic patient that thinks he is the King of France you do not sit there and try to find ways to alter reality to conform to his psychosis. At some point you have to come to grips with the fact that the person is crazy and that there is nothing that you can do about it. The same is true for people in the region that "hate us". When Arab moderates say that only a small population of Middle Easterners hates the West that is a boldfaced lie. I admit that only small segments of the population are terrorists, however one doesn't have to be a terrorist to hate the U.S. When there are groups of people burning the U.S. flag in the streets, I do not get the feeling that that is just a small minority. I know that the vast majority of Middle Easterners do not like the U.S. That is fine as far as I am concerned, they do not have to like us. However, any rational being would at least respect the country that is putting food on the table for their children.

To further understand why it is such a waste of time to win over the hearts and minds of terrorists it is useful to see, first hand, what makes them tick. Hezbollah, the terrorist group mentioned earlier, is a good example. Nasrallah is the leader of a terrorist group called Hezbollah that operates out of Lebanon. He recently said that, as far as the wholesale massacre Syria's government is committing to its civilian population, he backs Assad who is Syria's dictator. The reason he does that is because Assad gives him weapons. Nasrallah does not care about his fellow Muslims, including women and children, being slaughtered on a mass scale in the streets of Syria. All he cares about is getting weapons to kill people. There has never been a clearer example that terrorist groups do not care about the welfare of their own people, and all they care about is violence and murder. Hezbollah's main enemy is Israel yet Israel, has never killed Palestinians with the same volume and frequency as Syrians are killing their civilians every day. These terrorist groups try to act like they represent the common man, or common Muslim, who is being led astray by the West. However, when their people are facing possibly the biggest all out and brutal massacre in their recent history, the situation in Syria, they support the fascist Syrian government. This is a perfect example of just how fake and artificial these terrorists are. It is impossible and a waste of time to try to win over the minds of ruthless bloodthirsty killers that only care about murder.

The real answer to why many in the Arab World and Iran do not like us is rather simple. The reason they do no like us is because we are the most powerful country in the world and the most powerful country in the world has always been hated throughout history. It doesn't matter who they are. When the Roman Empire was rolling, the world hated them. When Napoleon was flourishing, all of Europe hated France. When the British Empire was reigning, the world hated them. When the U.S.S.R and the U.S.A were the most powerful countries, the entire world hated both. Naturally when the U.S.S.R fell there was a vacuum and the people disliked the U.S. more than usual. Whether they like us or not, is not and should not be anyone's concern, the question we should be asking is do we like them (terrorists), and the obvious answer is absolutely not. I do not like people that fly planes into buildings and kill innocent countrymen of mine. It is that simple. To change the mentality that creates terror, we must not do anything differently to make them like us. Changes need to be made to the modalities of the Middle Eastern governments themselves.

Despots and dictators rule Muslim countries in the Middle East. This is the reason there are terrorists in these countries. Home grown terrorists in democracies are very rare. The people in these countries live like animals and they do not have any human rights. The way the despots and dictators stay in power is by blaming the circumstances their people live in on someone other than themselves. They blame America, who incidentally is the biggest purchaser of their main export (oil), and Israel, the only real established democracy in the region. In response to this the masses let the government strip them of their last and most important possession: their lives. When individuals have nothing to live for, because of the way a government is set up, it is probably easy to decide to kill yourself, especially if someone genuinely believes in an amazing afterlife. Therefore democracy seems to be the only and ideal way for these countries to start changing the prevailing philosophy that breeds terror.

These dictators and kings are generally not good to their people. When their people have problems, like unemployment or poverty, the dictators and kings give them bogus reasons involving Americans on why they are suffering. The reason their people are suffering is because their own fascist leaders are taking all their people's money. So they blame it on Israel and the U.S., as if these countries magically are to blame for Arabs' problems. Because America spends so much money on oil in this area (see best customer analogy) it would be assumed that they would respect us and not be so moronic to think that the one group that provides them with cash is their problem. The reason we went into Iraq was to create a democracy and reverse this type of idiotic thought process. Democracy is the answer for the Middle East and this form of government will greatly reduce and someday eradicate the mindset that creates terrorists.

How many terrorists are citizens of democracies? Even foreign-born Arabs who have become citizens of democracies rarely become terrorists. I have never heard of an Arab American citizen who has committed any sort of terrorism. Close to half of the cab drivers in Chicago and New York are Arabs, however you never hear of them strapping on a bomb and detonating it in a mall (like the brand of terrorism committed against Israelis). The reason is that they feel like they have a chance at life. If terrorism is to be eradicated, it is necessary to restore hope in the people of the Middle East. The Bush administration felt that creating a democracy would do just that. Indirectly the noble goal of this war was to eradicate terrorism by creating a society where merit and not hate and murder is rewarded. For the critics that say there were not any terrorists in Iraq, they do not see the big picture. The point was to create a democracy in a country the administration felt had the resources to sustain it, in the hopes that the entire region could use that as an example (as will be discussed later, Egypt, Libya, and Syria are proof that this example worked). The fact that there were not any terrorists there should be seen as a positive; that theoretically would make it easier to set up a democracy than doing it in a country infested with terrorists. We must do everything we can to support and stimulate democracy in the Middle East. If the terrorists really want us out of their lives, blow up the oil fields. If not fight for democracy and vote yourself in, so we can fight like men. This way the scum of the earth will not attack our women and children and we will obliterate them. As God is my witness, we will destroy the terrorist movement in this world.

My problem isn't with the people and I know that they feel so hopeless that they feel that groups like Hamas and Hezbollah, with their funding of schools and hospitals and numerous other civil projects, are their only way out. But these groups use them like pawns and train the most desperate to give up their ultimate human right-the right to be alive-in suicide style attacks. The region can never prosper and be safe with groups such as these in leadership roles. The basic mentality that both Hamas and Hezbollah operate on is the Iranian model. Iran has used the right wing radical Islamic model for the past 30 years and they are proving to be a failed state. Iran is ripe for a people's revolution. Iran is a country with lots of oil and commerce and intelligent people including attorneys, engineers, and doctors. Before Khomeni, the leader of the Islamic Revolution, the Shah (their king before the revolution) was also a joke but at least he was progressive in certain aspects. Iran had a progressive society and they cannot even thrive under a right wing Islamic Radical leadership. If Iran with all its resources, relatively strong military, and very educated people cannot thrive under the radical Islamic model politically, Gaza and Lebanon surely cannot either.

Israel

Our only true complete allies, our real best friends, are England and Israel. There are too many Americans who do not understand that Israel is our ally and that we must do everything in our power to support them. After the cold war no American can deny that the Middle East has been our greatest cause of unrest. Desert Storm, 9/11, and the invasions of Afghanistan and Iraq prove this. Israel is our only ally in the region. This is why they are so crucial to our interests. In every war that Israel has had (which will be described later in this section) they have done exactly what the U.S. has told them to. That is the sign of a true ally. No other ally in our history has done that. In many of Israel's wars they had the power and capacity to completely neutralize their enemy, but they were always forced to stop because it was politically expedient for America's foreign policy to make them stop. During Desert Storm Iraq sent scud missiles to Israel, a country that had nothing to do with the war. The first President Bush asked Israel to not respond and, although they could have obliterated Iraq, they did not. A country knows it can trust an ally, when the ally does everything the country says.

Another less talked about reason that we must support Israel is their nuclear capability. Israel has the nuclear capacity to annihilate every major oil field in the Middle East. If this ever happened it could and would spin the entire world into mass chaos. If it seems the oil crisis is bad now, imagine what it would be if 2/3 of the world's oil supply vanished in a second. There would be the same demand and no supply and the entire world economy would crash; it would make the crash of 1929 look like pre-school. Now more than ever this scenario is becoming more of a reality due to Iran's pursuit of a nuclear weapon. If Iran sent nuclear bombs to Israel, Israel would rightfully use the nuclear option.

In discussing Israel's potential destruction, its origin must be analyzed. In the late 19th century many European Jews started practicing Zionism. Zionism means that all Jews should go back to Israel. To turn their vision into reality, people who believed in this started buying up land in what is now Israel. Then it was known as Palestine, which is a name the Romans gave the land; it had nothing to do with any former Arab country. Palestine was never an Arab controlled country; other countries always controlled them. While the Zionists continued buying land, the Second World War broke out and 6 million Jews were murdered. Other European Jews who survived were displaced. Many of the displaced Jews fled to Israel.

In 1948 the United Nations decided that approximately half of the land would be given to Jews and the other half to the Palestinians (including what they now want). After the announcement that created Israel, the Arab countries got up and walked out of the United Nations in a joint act of defiance. Following the United Nations vote in

1948, there was a Declaration of Independence by Israel. Compared to the land in the Middle East that was controlled by Muslim kings and dictators, Israel would have the right to have the equivalent to half of a matchstick in a football field of land. The Arab countries could not stomach the fact that the Israelis would have any land at all, so Arab armies from five countries invaded Israel. This resulted in Israel's War of Independence.

The Arab countries had organized armies and air forces with sophisticated weaponry. They also far outnumbered the Jews. Regardless, the rag-tag Jewish army won decisively. During the war the Egyptians told the Palestinians to leave their land, wait until the war was over and then come back after an Arab victory. Because that victory never happened many of these Palestinians were not allowed to come back, as they should not have been. Between the years of 1948–1952, there were 650,000 Palestinian refugees. Most fled from Israel to Arab states and were confined to refugee camps. Since that time these Palestinian refugees have not had a home. However, what the media never talks about is that the War of Independence indirectly created more Jewish refugees than Palestinian refugees. Between 1948 and 1952, 800,000 Jews were kicked out from Arab countries like Iraq and Egypt. These Jewish refugees had been living there for hundreds of years in their respective countries and were expelled because their countries' leaders wanted to punish Jews who had nothing to do with Israel. Most of these refugees were absorbed by Israel.

In 1956 Egypt cut off Israel's shipping from the rest of the world, by taking over the Suez Canal. No country can survive without shipping. So, therefore, in 1956, after a war with the Egyptians, Israel took over the Suez Canal. U.S. and Soviet pressure forced Israeli withdrawal from the canal; in exchange the U.S. guaranteed to protect Israel's shipping in the future. In 1967 Egypt once again sent troops to the Suez Canal and blocked Israel's shipping. The U.S. broke its promise and did not come to the aid of the Israelis. The situation was the catalyst for the most miraculous and decisive military victory of the century: the Six Day War. Israel destroyed and demoralized Syria, Jordan, and Egypt in six days. In less than a week Israel annihilated 15,000 troops, over 2,880 tanks and 810 aircraft. Israel captured the Sinai and Gaza, Judea and Samaria, and the Golan Heights. Before the war Jerusalem was split into east and west, and after the war it was reunited. Since that time Israel has given land and signed peace treaties with Egypt and Jordan. This has shown that it is possible for there to be peace and mutual respect between Muslim and Israeli.

All of Israel's history demonstrates that this entire time they have been defending their very existence, and that they have never done anything that could be mildly interpreted as betraying the U.S. Israel has even helped us against our former biggest enemy in the Middle East: Iraq. In 1981 they sent the air force to bomb Sadam Hussein's nuclear project. If they had not done that, it is very likely that he would have had nuclear weapons during operation Desert Storm and we would be living in a very different world right now.

Now there must be a solution to the Palestinian problem. I suggest that Jordan take an active role and assist with the problem. Jordan is basically Arab Palestine. None of the Arab countries, with the exception of Egypt, existed as such until the British, who controlled the area, created them; these are not countries like the countries in Europe that have existed for long periods of time. Jordanians and Palestinians are the same type of people; they became different when the British Empire put an arbitrary line between them, based on British economic and political interests. It would be as if, in the future, someone took over the U.S. and split us up between east and west, creating two countries. We would all still be Americans. This is the situation with Jordanians and Palestinians. Therefore, the solution to the Palestinian problem is for Jordan to create a federation with the West Bank and Gaza and that might be the end of the Palestinian problem. Jordan probably would not want any part of this, although Jordan's Queen Noor is Palestinian and very sympathetic to the Palestinian cause. The U.S. and Israel could make the offer appetizing to King Hussein by offering economic and military aid. For King Hussein it would be a huge public relations coup. He could prove in a very tangible way just how much he cares about the Palestinians.

The Palestinians, through their longest and most recognized leadership organization, the Palestinian Leadership

Organization (the "PLO"), have proven time and again that they are not capable of governing themselves. From violations of the Oslo accords, a treaty between Israel and the PLO, to abusing any trust that has been given to them, to involving themselves in terrorism, they simply cannot do it. In the latest democratic elections the Palestinians elected a terrorist group, Hamas, to lead them. That is the equivalent to a country electing Al-Qaeda to lead them politically. Imagine if Canada did that, being so close to the U.S.; that is basically what the Palestinians did to Israel. Because the Palestinians do not know how to behave themselves, Jordan would have to discipline them. Jordan has experience with this type of work. In 1970 when Palestinians lived in Jordan the PLO, once again, squandered an opportunity of good will in a disgusting classless manner and attempted to overthrow the Jordanian government. In a situation known as "Black September" the Jordanians wiped out more Palestinians in a month than Israel ever has in all of their conflicts with the Palestinians. The average American knows nothing about Black September, but they think they know about how Israelis murder Palestinians. This is because Arabs killing Arabs doesn't sell newspapers. It is almost like how black on black crime doesn't get much coverage in the United States, but if a white person kills a black person or vice versa that receives much more press coverage. Just like if an Israeli kills a Palestinian this receives much coverage.

If the Jordanians are not amiable to the plan I have outlined, there is another way to solve the Palestinian issue.

Israeli leadership could find the defensive positions needed from the territories they would be giving up to the Palestinians in some type of way. From that they could come up with a map their leading political parties are comfortable with. There would be no negotiations, just unilaterally mark up the land with no talks to the other side. Next, Israeli leadership would select a starting date and for every Israeli life killed due to a terrorist attack, Israel would take a square mile of that land back once and for all. For every month that goes by with no terrorist attack give the Palestinians a square mile. If the miles start stacking in Israel's favor, deport any Palestinian living in that particular bulk of land. This gives a peace plan and tangible consequences to terrorism. The simplicity of this plan is compelling. However, the ideal solution would involve bilateral talks between Israelis and Palestinians. That would be the best way to do it if it is possible.

The best way for peace is direct talks between Israelis and Palestinians, no one else, and no other way diplomatically. The Palestinian UN situation is so silly on a logical level. Imagine if a guy (Israel) owned a whole bunch of land and he was protecting it with force, regardless of how he got it, and in my mind I (the Palestinians) thought that I had all the justifications in the world to some of it. If that guy was willing to sit down and discuss it with me with no pre-conditions and only he had the power to give some up, would I get a bunch of my friends (the UN) to agree that I do own some and start trouble in a fantasy world or would I sit down with the owner and talk? No matter what the UN says, Israel has the power and they decide what is happening there, that is just the reality of the situation.

If viewed through an abstract lens, personal biases aside, these are facts. Anything the UN does at this point, on that issue, just adds to their already mounting complete irrelevance. Israel has the power to give the Palestinians a state, no one else, and definitely not the UN. Regardless of how anyone feels about it that is the reality on the ground. Therefore it would be prudent for both sides to sit down and start peace talks again not this UN buffoonery. I know that the UN gave the Israelis and the Palestinians a state in 1948, but it is a different real world now. Both sides must come together and talk and I do think the Palestinians should get a state in some type of way, shape, or form, but the UN is not the way. I think we are at a point where no one needs any more empty symbolic gestures. If the Palestinians want to speak to the Israeli Prime Minister, he is about 30 minutes away from them, not in New York (where the United Nations is located).

And again it should be firmly understood that solving the Israeli/Palestinian conflict will not be a panacea for the Arab World. Every single problem the Arab world and Iranians have, they will still have regardless of what happens with the Israelis and Palestinians. Women still won't be able to drive in Saudi Arabia, in Syria people and innocent children will continue to be murdered, and the Iranian system will still be dirty and corrupt. They will still have a completely regressive society, and they will continue to work on a nuclear bomb. Certain Arab dictators and kings will continue to take all the oil money for themselves and keep their people down. Do not be naive. The country that benefits the most from peace with the Palestinians is ironically Israel because they can stop with all the world media bias against them and finally move on with their lives. Israel has nuclear weapons at this point and it is not 1948 anymore. If they were the animals that much of the world claims they are, they could permanently end all the Palestinians in a matter of minutes, regardless of how anyone feels about it that is the truth. Sit down and talk and get it done, for the sake of everyone. The time for empty symbolic gestures, the UN song and dance, is over. All the UN does concerning this matter is create artificial drama in a conflict that has enough of that for a million lifetimes.

The entire Middle East crisis has been handled by just a lack of real world focus, real world problem solving, and real world vision. All sides share some of the blame, albeit in different amounts. I actually feel bad for the Palestinians because I wish they had a younger, well-educated, charismatic, visionary, leader that could unite the different factions in their group and that knew how to get things done-in the interests of peace-in the real world. A true real human partner for peace is what I mean. We are a whole new generation of people and I think we can do things the older generations just could not, that is actually called evolution and it is the way things progress, historically speaking.

President Clinton offered the Palestinians a really great deal, some said the best they would ever get in 2000, and they turned it down. Some say, the Palestinian leader at the time, Arafat, turned it down because he was scared that his own people would have murdered him for accepting the deal. I think a real leader should be willing to risk everything for his people. Arafat was no Sadat. Sadat was Egypt's leader when they accepted a historic peace treaty with Israel in the late 1970s. Many say that a similar deal with the Palestinians cannot happen because Israel is such a violent country that has no restraint.

As far as this no restraint from the Israelis we always hear about, do some research into how Russia handles terrorism. Like I said, the U.S. sold and fought a war where they killed hundreds of thousands of civilians (who had nothing to do with terrorism) because they got attacked, in a proportionally much weaker way than Israel has been attacked by terrorism. In all of Israel's wars with Arabs (5 wars), from the War of independence to the ill fated Lebanon campaign, they have not killed the amount of people that the U.S. has in its current war against terror. Read that sentence again. What other country has enough nuclear power to destroy every oil field in the Middle East and continues to let its people be murdered by terrorism? Israel has no restraint? Israel is the definition of restraint. Israel has the power to destroy all of their enemies in a matter of minutes and they do not even think about using the nuclear option. If that is not restraint, I do not know what is.

The Turkish Prime Minister called Israeli soldiers defending themselves and killing 9 people a "bloody massacre" in regards to the Gaza flotilla situation a couple of years ago. What happened with the Gaza flotilla is that there was a small boat and Israeli commandoes boarded the ship to check its contents and they encountered violence (which is on video tape) so they defended themselves. The reason they have to check everything that comes into Gaza is because a terrorist group controls Gaza politically so they could be importing arms and weapons to use in terrorist acts. What would the American Coast Guard do if a boat bringing aid to Quebec was run by Al-Qaeda? They would check for contraband and they would defend themselves if attacked by the crew. If that is a bloody massacre what is the Turks slaughtering 1.5 million Armenians at the beginning of the 20th century in a disgusting repulsive act of genocide? Turkey's leaders never took responsibility for that or even offered up a public apology. If a country is responsible for something much worse, like the Turkish against the Armenians, that they didn't take responsibility for, then it is in no position to criticize a much more defensible action against a much smaller amount of people (Israel against Gaza flotilla) it is hypocrisy.

Another example would be if Germany never took responsibility or apologized for the holocaust (which in reality they did ad nauseam) and then years later some Palestinians killed some Jews in a clear act of self defense, that was on video, imagine if Germany would then come out and say that that was a bloody massacre. Is the hypocrisy visible? To me the fundamental truth is that Jewish life has never been valued as much as non-Jewish life by the international community, for whatever reason. That is the fundamental problem. Therefore when Jewish life is lost or when Jewish life is defended, it really doesn't matter to most people, in fact they do not care or they get really angry when Jewish lives are saved at the expense of other people's lives (whoever those other people are, including terrorists in many cases). Again because why should a life be saved at the expense of another that is worth more (in their eyes)?

Some say that the violence by Palestinians is justifiable because of the conditions in Gaza. In comparison to Gaza, conditions in the West Bank are much better. If the Israelis were out to oppress the Palestinians why wouldn't they treat the West Bank exactly the same? The reason is that Hamas does not dominate the West Bank and they are not in charge there. Terrorism has been less frequent in the West Bank, so Israel does not have to take extreme measures to defend themselves there. When the Palestinians were given control of Gaza if they would have said we recognize Israel and we will be peaceful, the conditions would not be "inhuman" as many people say, but quite the opposite. The difference between Hamas and Israel is that Hamas are a terrorist organization and Israel is not. Sure Hamas funds schools, hospitals, and other civil projects, probably one of the reasons that the Palestinian people support them so much. But that would be the same as a serial killer claiming that he should have amnesty because he has donated a lot of money to charity. The two things have nothing to do with each other and one doesn't absolve you of the other. A terrorist is someone who specifically targets civilians to advance a political cause. Israel does not target school buses, shopping malls, and the like. Granted, when Israel attacks there is collateral damage and loss of civilian life and that is too bad, but it is the reality of war. Israel drops pamphlets into the territories before they attack, telling civilians that they are coming. No terrorist groups do that. It is against the spirit of what terrorism is.

I wish some Palestinians would understand, now some probably do, that they can have land and the Israeli military would protect them. They do not even need an army, they could entirely focus on raising their children, strengthening their economy, and working good jobs. What they need is a state of the art soccer program in their territory. Those things are what life is about. But they need Israel and Israel needs the Palestinians for peace. If there was peace money would flow in from the international community to build their territory and sponsor a state of the art soccer program. Wouldn't families rather watch their kids play soccer than watch them die in a fruitless pursuit? Regardless of the past the reality on the ground is that Israel is not going any-where. And yes the Palestinians are not going anywhere either and that needs to be accepted to move on as well. If there was peace, Israel itself would give money to the Palestinian territories to build, along with the Saudis and most Middle Eastern countries. Israel's economy is doing great right now and they are generating tons of money. If peace is achieved, it would be their responsibility to donate lots of aid to the territories.

After all the years of heartache and being led by leaders that just want violence, regardless of all justifications they have claimed, the Palestinian people deserve peace of mind and soul and most importantly a bright future for their children. I know that there are many Palestinians that want something like this, and I have spoken to many personally here in the U.S. If there was peace Israel could sign peace treaties with all the Middle Eastern countries in the future, the dictators won't be around much longer, so this is possible. Then finally the people of the Middle East united can be real players in world politics, the world economy and they can have their voices heard and have a real seat at the table. Instead of this money for favors nonsense that is currently the situation with most Middle Eastern countries. The key is democracy, friendship, and mutual respect.

These are terms to any peace deal with the Palestinians, Israel will not negotiate with terrorists (Hamas) unless there is a genuine sign of good faith, they will never go back to the 1967 borders, there will never be a right of return for refugees, Jerusalem will never be split, and any "independent state" the Palestinians get will be totally demilitarized and under military protection of Jordan, Israel, or NATO. This is the reality that Hamas and the PLO helped create.

For years I've heard Presidential speeches regarding the Israeli Palestinian conflict. They make for nice flowery sound bites, but the reality is that none of those speeches matter or ever make a difference. These speeches always tend to give fleeting consternation to Israel and false hope to Palestinians. Israel is a sovereign nation and it will do whatever it wants. The world should get past the denial aspect and should come to accept this. If the U.S. doesn't pull aid to Pakistan after they quartered Bin Laden for years, I doubt Israel's aid is in jeopardy under any scenario. If the U.S. wants to tell someone what to do, tell Syria and Iran what to do.

However, on a completely different scale, Israel does have some domestic problems that should be changed. In Israel the only marriages recognized are religious marriages. Meaning that Jewish citizens have to get married by a rabbi, Christians by a priest, etc. So the people who are atheists or agnostic, or do believe but just do not want a religious wedding have to succumb to the will of other very religious people who have nothing to do with their lives. In Israel a judge cannot marry individuals. That is absolutely absurd. Israel holds itself to be the most progressive and modern democracy in the Middle East, but they do not give the Israeli people, who sacrifice their youth fighting and defending the country, a basic right like that? Religion is important and has a very special place in Israel, but it should not be forced on anyone in a democracy, in any way. People who risk their lives for their country, most Israelis are forced to serve in the army, should be able to decide what they want to do when it comes to a choice as personal as marriage. That law should be changed. I do believe in God and I would be okay with a religious wedding for myself, if the circumstances were right, but I say this to show that I am not bringing this up for myself. Rather it is for the people and it is one of my guiding principles. When it comes to social policy, citizens should be able to do what they want, but no one should tell others what they have to do.

Religion in Israel is also a problem when it comes to military service. In Israel there are very religious Jewish people who do not work and their children are the only Israelis who do not have to do military service. Every other Israeli person has to work, pay taxes in part to support the very religious who study torah all day, and they have to send their children to the military. What the very religious get is the equivalent of unemployment checks. The situation is totally unfair. The very religious use the excuse that because the messiah has not arrived that they do not recognize Israel, but they do recognize and spend the money that Israeli taxpayers give them. Interesting how that works. The reason the bigger political parties do not have the courage to take them on is that they represent about 16 seats in the Knesset (Israeli Congress) that are needed to pass any laws in the coalition-style governing that Israel has. Israel should immediately stop any government payment to the very religious and force their kids to do military service. In New York we have very religious Jews that have real jobs and earn their money. They do not live off the government like parasites. Imagine in the U.S. if the Christian Right did not have to work and were supported by the taxpayers to read the bible all day. Further imagine if every American had to join the military from age 18 to 21 except for the Christian Right. What goes on in Israel, on that front, is politics at its worst. If the very religious Jewish people do not recognize Israel, Israel should not recognize them.

An also absurd situation is that in the wake of the mortgage crisis in the U.S., to buy a home in Israel the people have to put 40% down. They do not want the mortgage crisis that happened in the U.S. to happen in Israel. In theory I like the idea because it is a preemptive measure that protects the system by ensuring that people who buy homes will not end up in foreclosure. But young people, who have done nothing wrong, are being punished for the mistakes of the U.S. and just cannot afford it. Also, wealthy European tourists and investors (especially the French) buy up condos in Israel for vacation homes so the demand is still high in the real estate market. In Israel men and women give up years of their precious youth (18–21 for men, 18–20 for women) to risk their lives and serve their country in the military. Israel is not just a country of citizens, it is a country of veterans.

These veterans deserve better standards and should never take a backseat to wealthy foreigners. This is especially true when it interferes with the Israelis ability to own homes. The solution is a compromise for the younger generations who cannot afford homes under the current system. If you are 40 years old or younger and you have a very high credit score, you should only have to put 25% down. The actual number isn't important just something considerably lower than the current 40%. That could be a game changer for people in need. An issue that affects Israel and the Israeli people and that is caused by the international community, not Israel, is the location of embassies in Israel.

In every country in the world the embassies are all in their respective capital cities. In the U.S. they are in D.C., in France they are in Paris, and in Argentina they are in Buenos Aires, etc. Jerusalem is the capital of Israel, however all the embassies are in Tel Aviv (more modern other main city). The reason this is done is because certain people and countries in the international community are offended that Jerusalem is Israel's capital. Most Arabs believe that Jerusalem belongs to them and they do not recognize it as the capital of Israel. Most do not even recognize Israel as a country, much less Jerusalem as the capital. Israel needs to move all their embassies to Jerusalem. Reality is reality, and Jerusalem is the capital of Israel. Any country that has a problem with that can cut diplomatic ties with Israel. It is an insult to the entire nation of Israel that the world forces them to play this game acting like Jerusalem is not the capital in every single way. Jerusalem is the capital and that is where the embassies should be. If not, then Israel should choose to put their embassies overseas wherever they want. Fair is fair and that is how the international community is treating Israel.

Iran

Iran is not like the Arab countries that England basically invented and hand picked despots to rule over them. Iran/Persia is a country that has been around for at least 2,500 years. This makes them extremely dangerous because they have a strong national identity. Countries that have been around for this long have a tendency to stay strong; it is usually not a coincidence that they have existed for so long. To understand the context of the Iran situation and try to figure out how we ended up where we are now, it is important to highlight some important Iranian historical developments vis a vis the United States.

In the early 1950s the Iranians democratically elected a prime minister whose name was Mossadeq. He was doing and saying certain things that were against American interests, but nothing that he said was nearly as bad as what the Ayatollah and Ahmadinejad have done since. He simply wanted Iranians to have more economic independence. The U.S. and England saw him as a destabilizing factor and they devised a plan to have him overthrown; eventually he was. The Shah (king of Iran), sponsored by the U.S. and England, replaced him. The Iranian people were very angry with this, as they should have been. The United States should never have anything to do with overthrowing democratically elected leaders, unless those leaders are terrorists or represent terrorist groups. This gentleman did not.

In the 1960s there were many Americans in Iran for business and strategic reasons. We were in the midst of the cold war. Iran is geographically very close to Russia. Iran was looked at as the dominant power in the Middle East; therefore our foreign policy interest was to ensure that they did not become communists. In 1962, the United States tried to pass an immunities bill in Iran that would guarantee legal immunity for all U.S. government personnel in Iran. This means that an American could commit any crime in Iran, including theft and murder, and he could not be prosecuted. The Iranian public was rightfully and justifiably very upset about this. I believe all such policies granting diplomatic immunity should be done away with. The way that this particular problem should be treated is that the foreign country where the diplomat is stationed must guarantee that the diplomat will be tried in a court of a predetermined third country that both countries agree to. Then he should serve his sentence in his country of origin. This seems like a fair compromise.

In 1979 Iran's king, who was friendly with the U.S., was displaced by a revolution led by Islamic radicals. These radicals believed that Muslim Shia Law, a very conservative and oppressive form of religious law, should rule the government. Iran basically stripped their people of all their human rights in the process of executing the imposition of Shia law. After the Iranian revolution during

Iran's war with Iraq, the religious fanatics who hijacked the country gave young kids (thirteen and fourteen year olds) keys to wear around their necks. Then they would send these kids to minefields and they told them that the keys would send them to the afterlife. They were encouraged to take part in suicide missions. Political prisoners who fought against the Shah but did not agree with the religious fanatics were thrown in jail, beaten, raped (women), and often executed. The government came up with a solution that they either had to say that they agree with the current administration or face execution. As a result, tens of thousands of people were executed. Under Islamic law a virgin cannot be killed, so if a young woman, who is a virgin, has different political views or does not agree with the government before she is murdered, government officials rape the woman and then kill her.

These radicals went to the American embassy and took 52 American hostages and held them for 444 days. These Americans were tortured for the entire time. International law states that diplomats must never be harmed in a foreign country. The Iranians who participated in these actions are animals and should never be forgiven. Iranians constantly complain that Americans have treated them badly, but nothing that the Americans have done has compared to taking 52 foreign service workers hostage and torturing them. Ahmadinejad, the current Iranian President, was one of the torturers. That alone is a valid reason for the U.S. never to speak to him. President Jimmy Carter should have told them that if they did not give up the hostages within 24 hours, we would destroy a major city in Iran without saying which one. Then if they harmed the hostages, we would assure them that the entire families of the Iranians involved would be killed and that we would drop a nuclear bomb on Tehran. Just because we would use the threat doesn't mean that we would do it, air strikes could have been sufficient. Giving them 24 hours to decide puts them in frantic mode; if given a month, then they can really analyze their options. Instead, Carter negotiated with terrorists. Carter's milquetoast reaction to a bunch of students taking American hostages emboldened the Islamic Radicals and set the stage for the world we live in now. These lunatics stood up to the U.S., embarrassed us and, to this day, suffered no real consequences. Carter even agreed to bar the American hostages from filing international lawsuits against Iran. Iran has done a lot more to us than our other "enemies".

The Soviet Union never took American hostages neither did Iraq for that matter. I was not against the Iraq war, but I always thought that we should have been going after Iran instead. Every reason we stated of why we were going after Iraq applies to Iran. They are the biggest state sponsor of terrorism. They openly fund Hamas, Hezbollah, and the Taliban, and they also house Al-Qaeda. The weapons of mass destruction argument also applies to them, as they are working on a nuclear bomb. They also aided the Iraqi insurgents who killed many Americans in the war there. We want to spread everything that represents progress for humanity: human rights, women's rights, freedom of religion, and democracy. They want to spread everything that represents regression: terror, no freedom of religion, and violent oppression.

Sometimes in life there is real evil and there are not two sides to a story. Regarding Iran, this is particularly true. Just like most civilized individuals can agree that Hitler was evil, the same can be said about Iran and the power structure there. They said that the Holocaust did not take place and that they will blast Israel out of existence. They are close to getting a nuclear weapon. The solution to this problem is to send the air force (American or Israeli) to blow up their nuclear installations or give them a nuclear ultimatum. First, pick an area that is not that populated and say that a nuclear bomb will be dropped there if they do not abandon their nuclear program. Concurrently send the air force to bomb the reactors. Just like what we should have done when they took hostages. If countries do not respect us enough not to take hostages and take part in terrorism against us, then we must force them to be terrified of us so they won't do it. Our first priority is for them not to manifest any aggression against us. We need to reach that end in whatever form we can; we cannot always be "nice".

As was discussed earlier in the Israel section, if Iran were to send a nuclear bomb to Israel, Israel would nuke all the oil fields in the Middle East and that would spin the world's economy into complete and utter chaos. Regardless of where individuals stand on Israel, people should care about their security for that reason alone.

Christians should care about Iran's aggression for religious reasons. Jesus Christ was a Jew. That means that his only true relatives and the people who beyond a shadow of a doubt share his blood are Jews, specifically Sephardic Jews that have never left Israel. The second coming, in the eyes of Christians, depends on Jesus returning to Israel and when he returns, according to the gospel, all the Jews will convert to Christianity. For Christians who believe this, how is that supposed to happen if Iran blows up Israel? Think of the religious consequences of Ahmadinejad having a bomb and destroying Israel as he states that he will.

Countries like Iran complain that we helped Iraq in the Iraq vs. Iran war. What they and others that constantly complain about us "changing sides" continually and doing whatever benefits us must understand is that this has been happening since the beginning of modern countries. For example, France helped the United States during the revolution for the sole reason that England was against us and the French despised the English and were at an almost constant state of war with them. More recently Mossadeq was a democratically elected leader who the U.S. took out of power. Soon after Kennedy attempted a Cuban invasion, that failed miserably, and he successfully backed a coup in Iraq that put the Baathists (Sadam Hussein's political party) in power. He did all of this in three years. The point is that it is a political reality that powerful countries switch sides and back coups in other countries all the time. The Iranians need to understand how superpowers work, as this has always been the case. As long as there are countries, they will continue to do things that benefit themselves, and quite frankly that is exactly what they should do. Iranians held American citizens in Iran for over a year and tortured them. The least we can do is give military support to any country fighting against them. They are lucky we did not destroy Tehran.

The long-term solution to the Iranian problem is that the Persian people must take steps to overthrow the Iranian government. It must be a grass roots movement with American economic and arms support. We must contact every single Persian ex-patriot around the world and try to get them to support the Free Persia movement. Whether they want to return to the country or not is irrelevant. At the very least we could use their financial support. We should figure out how much money a war with Iran would cost over the next five years and take half that amount and use it to fund the Free Persia movement. With the advent of the internet we have a rich pool of innovative resources that we can tap to reach our goal. We must contact every single Iranian on "myspace.com", "facebook.com", and "twitter.com" and lobby them to join the movement. Also, consult with all the email providers in this country and get the emails of every single person in Iran. Then we need to start feeding them information and let them know that there is hope. Ask if they want to help the movement. Tell them to set up bogus email accounts so they can freely communicate with us. They could go to internet cafes and get it done.

The internet is a resource that the corrupt Iranian leadership cannot control. We need to use computer software that has the power to mask who the Persians are talking to, so the government won't crack down. We must build a virtual army. The Persian ex-pats, students, and workers are the future of Persia. The name Iran should be changed to Persia, which is incidentally the real name of these historically successful people. Their progress has been hijacked for the past thirty years. Every single day that goes by with their current leadership is a waste of time. When the CIA stated that Iraq had weapons of mass destruction, I did not see people rushing to believe them. Now the CIA states that Iran does not have nuclear weapons and most people are rushing to believe them and take them at their word. Why is that? The CIA has been weak and in a state of disarray since President Bill Clinton cut spending on the agency and imposed ridiculous rules, such as not letting anyone with a criminal record be a source.

We need to end the Iranian regime for many reasons, not just because they are trying to develop nuclear weapons. Most of the young Persians love our way of life. They listen to our music, they follow our sports, and behind closed doors at home they live like Westerners. Iran went from the most progressive country in the Middle East, before 1979, to one of the least. More people, proportionally, had cars, television, and they had the best educational centers in the Middle East. Now it is common in this self-described "virtuous" government that a young woman will be arrested for something as trivial as walking with a young man in public and then the police call the parents and only allow the daughter to leave custody after the parents pay a bribe. They do not even hide the fact or make it subtle, they state, "we have arrested your daughter for walking with a boy and it will cost $500.00 for us to let her go." They do such absurd things as outlawing neckties because according to them they are a sign of Western culture. Just as Ahmadinejad states that his country has no problem with the American people, he just has a problem with our leadership, I do not have a problem with the Persian people, in fact I am counting on them, I have a problem with their government. They are the ones that control the country's weapons, armies, money and resources. They will be dealt handled.

Another fact that should make the so-called left in the United States furious, which it does not, is that by law homosexuals receive capital punishment in Iran. That means that they are executed. In the U.S. homosexuals choose political parties based on which one supports them being able to be married. The fact that homosexuals cannot be married everywhere here is very important and considered to be a serious human rights infringement. However, in Iran they are killing the supposed homosexual brothers and sisters of American gays and the vast majority of U.S. citizens are vehemently against any military action in Iran. If people in the U.S. wanted to help people just like them, this would not be the case. That would be like Jews in the U.S. being against American involvement against the Nazis in World War II. The most pacifist of Jews would never feel that way, because Jews understand that their plight does not end where American borders end. Maybe it is possible that there are no homosexuals in Iran, as Ahmadinejad ridiculously stated when he came to Columbia University. His absurd government may have murdered all of them.

Imagine the Christian Right overthrowing our government in a violent revolution. Now imagine that the Christian Right began telling people what they must wear, stripping women of their rights, and making a law that all homosexuals and those who don't agree with them would be executed. There would be school prayer in all schools, public and private. The Bible and their interpretation of what is written therein would replace the law. Now imagine that while this happened the entire world just sat and watched and no one helped. Then after thirty years of this, we elected a president who continuously talked about Armageddon and the end of days, and how all of that was going to happen soon. Would we want that type of regime having access to a nuclear weapon? Substitute Christian Right with Radical Islam and that is what is happening. For women, things like showing a wrist, having a loud laugh, or having a walkman are considered grounds to be arrested. Again where is the feminist outrage in the U.S. over all of this? American women are so concerned about making exactly the same amount of money as men (as they should be) but they will not raise a finger to help others who do not live in our country. Are American women really just in favor of equal rights for women in the U.S. or women in the entire world? Please stop being so provincial, now is the time. The heart and mind should not draw human made limitations, like borders, to universal concepts like equal rights for all.

The way a government treats their own citizens vis a vis human rights is the real indication of where they stand. Iran complains about how Israelis treat Palestinians, people who blow up and murder Israeli citizens. While at the same time, Iranians torture, murder, and rape their own citizens for infractions such as being a homosexual, a man wearing a tie, women not covering their heads and having different political or religious opinions. Israelis punish enemies based on their murderous actions; Iranians punish their citizens based on their thoughts and their harmless actions. The first is not only justifiable it is necessary. The second is both intolerable and sub-human. Diplomatically the United States should not meet with Ahmadinejad; it would weaken our legitimacy and credibility around the world and most importantly to our own citizens. He states that the Holocaust never happened and that Israel should be wiped off the face of the planet. Imagine if he said that slavery never happened and that Africa should be wiped off the face of the planet. The American public reaction to him would be much different.

We must first take every economic measure possible to squeeze Iran into submission. We must pressure every country that trades with them to do the same. For countries that are with us, we must reward them with beneficial trade packages. For countries that are against us, we must make our trade packages with them worse. This strategy is perfectly within our rights. Iran threatens to close the Straits of Hormuz, which would close off a big portion of oil that they currently export to the world. However, we have the proper ships nearby to make sure that this will not occur. If we do ultimately send diplomats to speak to Iran we would have some pre-conditions. Before speaking to Iran we would require each person involved in the hostage crisis to serve a jail sentence in the U.S. equal to the amount of time that Americans were held hostage. That wouldn't even be equal punishment because the American hostages were tortured and constantly threatened with execution. Many were held in solitary confinement. Carter handled it terribly, letting the situation disintegrate into one of the most embarrassing moments for the U.S., this led to the start of the Islamic Radical movement which we are still paying for today. Another pre-condition would be that Ahmadinejad would have to be out of power. It is simply unacceptable for us to speak to any world leader who states that the Holocaust never happened.

Finally, the most important pre-condition to any talks would be that they would have to agree to abandon their nuclear weapons program. Many countries that are sympathetic to Iran ask: if so many other countries can have nuclear weapons why can't Iran? The reason that Iran having a nuclear bomb is different from other countries having them is that they explicitly state that they are building it to destroy Israel. If Iceland said that they were building a nuclear bomb to wipe out New Zealand specifically, then the international community would take actions against them as well. This matter needs to be looked at in the abstract. Not only does Iran openly threaten Israel with a nuclear weapon, they are the number one state sponsor of terrorism. They support Hamas, Hezbollah, and Al-Qaeda. There is also a very realistic risk that a nuclear Iran would supply a terrorist group with nuclear capabilities in the future.

Persians have the chance now to rise against their leaders and be Persians once again! This is what the world needs. With rich culture, talents, and enthusiasm Persians could rejoin the world economy and become the China or India of their region as far as economic relevance. Do not let this opportunity pass by. The United States needs to gather all of the ex-patriots interested in helping their country and through covert operations infiltrate Iran and help the people. This is something the Persians, must do, but we will help. The revolution in Iran cannot be peaceful unfortunately. Their regime is made up of bloodthirsty and completely violent animals. They don't value the lives of their citizens at all and unlike the Egyptian government, they won't hesitate to murder their own people on a mass scale for demonstrating. Regardless, the brave freedom-yearning Persian people demonstrated in the streets. They are heroes.

The international intelligence community needs to find a way to get the people who want to overthrow the government arms, intelligence, and money. Iran is the head of the snake of Islamic Radicals. If we can spread the revolution there, we win and so do the Persian people and the Islamic Radical movement is done. Then there will be peace in the Middle East. Either now or later, this will happen. The highest priority for the CIA computer programmers is to keep social media outlets open in Iran. This is a peaceful thing that we can do from the United States to help. If the Islamic Radicals are no longer in charge of Iran and they get secular democracy, then that means they will no longer fund their proxies Hamas and Hezbollah. Consequently those two terrorist groups will disappear soon after.

Furthermore and most importantly we will no longer have to worry about the biggest threat to the security of the region and the world: a nuclear Iran. This is the opportunity of a lifetime. Iran's government praised Egypt's revolution, but when demonstrators took to the streets in Iran they called for the execution of demonstrators. Americans are unaware of this because, unlike Egypt, Iran prohibits foreign journalists and cameras inside their borders. There is no room in the modern world for the Iranian regime. The Persian people need all the peaceful help we can give.

Afghanistan

The leader of Afghanistan recently said that they would support Pakistan if we ever went to war with them. How many Americans have died and how much money have we dumped in Afghanistan to give them democracy? And this is how they repay us? That statement was a symbolic slap in the face by Afghanistan. After everything we've done what a total lack of respect. The U.S. needs to pull everybody we have there as soon as possible. Every single minute we are there is more money wasted that we could use to start paying off the Chinese debt. I want to get America's economic freedom back from the Chinese. This is like a player gambling at poker, losing all his money, and the dealer insulting the player. The player is in debt up to his neck and it is his money that keeps the casino in business. That is the analogy. What type of dupe would do that? Our foreign policy towards Afghanistan is that dupe. Many Americans who continue to support the Afghanistan campaign say that if we leave, the terrorists will come back there. If terrorists do organize in Afghanistan, after we leave, we can just bomb their camps with surgical specific strikes through our air power, we do not need ground troops there. They have made their feelings towards us crystal clear. If we did not need to invade Pakistan to take out Bin Laden, and their intelligence did not help us, we do not need ground troops or any Afghani intelligence to take out terrorists in the future there. Even if our economy had a surplus, unemployment was 2%, and the budget was completely balanced, I would say to get out immediately. Never waste money, no matter how much you have, especially and most importantly other people's money at the federal level.

Everyone knows that we will leave Afghanistan eventually. No matter when we leave, the consequences will be the same. Whatever will play out in Afghanistan, will play out regardless of when we leave. After we leave whatever government is left there will be very weak and in a precarious spot. Why waste money and time? It makes no sense and it is especially disgusting in light of the fact that we owe so much money, have so many unemployed people, and that we are in an economic crisis. If they really want democracy, they will have to do it themselves, like the other countries in Middle East are doing. Afghanistan does not have the relatively progressive society and wealth (oil) that Iraq does. They are two totally different situations, so similar strategies will not work the same in each place.

The Military

Right now we have an invasion-based military. This should be changed. We need to make homeland security the number one priority of all armed forces and then funnel money from army invasion-style spending and give it to the CIA, special forces, seals, rangers, and towards more of a specialized surgical strike military with the Navy, Air Force, and Army. Our CIA and special forces could be stronger than ever. Overall, I would cut the defense budget. One way I would do it is by cutting waste. For example, paying 1 extraordinary special forces soldier is better and cheaper than paying four average ones who are members of the army. The armed forces could shrink and as long as we make and buy more specialized weapons, jets, and drones, we could cut spending on tanks and manpower. It is no longer about manpower. Eventual secular democracies in the Middle East, where countries would have future peace treaties with Israel, would translate into spending cuts by the United States. These revolutions in the Middle East are so important for so many different reasons to us and the Muslim people.

All our wars, unless our existence is at stake, should be done by the airforce/navy jet fighters. Forget the ground troops method. The future is here and that is an antiquated way of doing things. Ground troops should be the last option in any confrontation, not the first.

I would also cut many of the military bases around the world on a case by case basis. For example our military base in Germany would be shut down. That base in particular is like a small city, and wastes a very high amount of taxpayer money every single day. World War II was a very long time ago. Western Europe, including Germany, is now a full ally of the United States, so there is no reason to keep a base there that is wasting money on a daily basis. This same rationale would be applied to every military base. At the same time certain very important and relevant bases would be kept. Our base in South Korea is one. They share a border with North Korea, which is one of the most unstable countries on earth, that has a very strong military and nuclear weapons. We must stay there to protect South Korea, a democracy and a firm ally of the United States.

Arab Awakening

For the first time in my life, when I see demonstrations in the Middle East, I do not see American flags burning, Israeli flags burning, Death to U.S.A signs, or Death to Israel signs. If that is not a sign for hope, I don't know what is. The Arab awakening from Egypt, to Libya, to Syria is demonstrating that the truth is finally winning in the Middle East. People now realize that the direct source of their problems with unemployment, poverty, and terrible quality of life, are the fascist dictators and kings that rule the region. For years their leaders have blamed the U.S. and Israel for all their countries' problems, while they themselves stole all the people's money. I never thought I'd live to see this ultimate revolution in the Middle East. But they cannot do it alone. We must form an international coalition and help any country in the Middle East that wants to free itself from their murdering, lying, and absolutely barbaric leaders. Forget that democracies in the region would help us tremendously in our geopolitical goals. We must help if only for humanitarian reasons.

Why is the American left so concerned about gay rights and animal rights, but when people are being slaughtered in Syria, for example, they do not care? How about human rights? They care more about animals and gays getting married than the lives of other human beings and I think that is wrong. Gays are not being killed for being gay in the United States, But Syrians are being killed just for wanting basic human rights. The same can be said about people from the opposite side of the spectrum in the U.S., the Christian Right. For the Christian Right in this country, God says a life is a life, correct? These lives being killed in Syria are not fetuses. They are actual human beings beyond the shadow of any doubt. Isn't that hypocrisy? Or is it that God is an American and only cares about American lives? The self described religious in this country act like that most of the time. You wonder why the world does not understand the United States sometimes. Innocent humans beings being killed fighting for democracy is the problem of every good person and democratic country in the world. That does not mean we should invade them, but we could completely cut them off and send our special forces and CIA to take out Assad. It is time for an ultimatum: leave or die. People are people and we are all in this together.

There were protests very recently in Syria and the day after the country's security forces went door to door to people's homes in the area and shot them dead. Here in the U.S. the lazy youth complain about the richest people in our country. In Syria they protest for rights as basic as freedom of speech and other human rights, and they are being slaughtered for it. Yet the world does nothing. Both what is happening to the innocent civilians and the reaction of the world, is gruesome and grotesque. The world has the power to stop it and they just do not. I would suggest a Mossad and CIA joint mission. Together they could form an assassination squad to take out Syria's dictator Assad. The killing squad can enter Syria through Israel, make a deal with a Syrian General, offer him money, land, and let him take over after their current leader is killed, until he can calm things down for democratic elections. In exchange have the General take responsibility for forming the coup and killing Assad. That way the Mossad and the CIA would be kept out of the press. The death of their ruthless dictator will appease the Syrian people for at least a year, while there can be a peaceful transition to democracy. These type of military operations are 1970s and 1980s style CIA missions, but for once we would be doing it for the right reasons.

The CIA used to do things like this to take out democratically elected leaders. For example they shot and killed a leader named Allende in Chile who was elected democratically. It is time we start protecting human beings, no matter where they are from, and give them the most basic rights that every human being must have. If not now, when? No need for invasions either, they wastes lives and money. It can all be done on the cheap, like Libya and the assassination squad idea. In a country like Syria a popular uprising is not enough, because the military there is much more strong and organized than the military was in Libya. Every individual revolution is different and requires its own particular strategy.

Again I am not naive, far from it. I know that there is a considerable chance that some of these countries, or all, will elect Islamic Radicals if they are given freedom and democracy. I am a bit conflicted, but I choose to believe in people and I must fight for democracy. If the citizens of countries that are fighting in the Arab Spring make the wrong decision and elect radicals, at least it is the truth of what they want. If it is an ultimate showdown that they want in the Middle East, they will get it, and lose in a horrifying manner. However, I hope they will choose real freedom, peace, prosperity and, most importantly, a bright future for their children. All Muslims have to do is compare countries like Iran to countries like the U.S., France, and other European countries. Are Muslims flocking to Iran or flocking to Europe these days? Muslim immigration in Europe is like Mexican immigration in the United States as far as volume. How are things going so far with the radicals in Iran compared to those other democratic free countries I mentioned? How is everything going on the human rights front in Iran? How does it feel to see children be used by the more powerful and seeing them die carrying out terrorist acts while murdering other people? People in the Middle East, Muslims: where would you rather live and raise your own children? Iran or the U.S. and Europe? With democracy, you will have the ability to take everything you like from the western world and integrate it into your own countries, while not including anything you don't like, as you preserve your culture, religious beliefs, and customs. Isn't that the ideal situation? The world and whatever you believe in above and beyond this world does not give chances like this everyday, or even for every generation for that matter. The world could have taken the safe route and backed all the dictators from Mubarak, to Khadafy, to

Assad, to maintain the status quo and be safe. But they created a golden opportunity in the interests of humanity and doing the right thing. What will be done with it?

In Egypt and Libya the revolutions were relatively peaceful and they both happened so fast. Who would have guessed years ago that Egypt and Libya would be free now? In Middle Eastern countries, before the internet and social media, they had no idea what the outside world was like. They used to believe all the lies, specifically that all of their problems were the fault of the Israelis and the Americans. For example, their leadership would tell their population that the reason the Arab people did not have money and lived in poverty was because of America and Israel. When the whole time the reason they had no money was because the evil dictators were taking all the wealth and the oil money for themselves, while stealing from their own people. It is rumored that Khadafy may have been the richest man on earth. In some cases their leaders encouraged their own people to kill themselves in terrorist acts to perpetuate the lies that kept them in power.

In Saudi Arabia they make women lead totally repressed lives, they cannot drive, while the royal family has tons of vacation homes. For example, in Spain the Saudi Royals have vacation homes where the royal women act how they want. The way women are treated there is terrible and it really is hurting the people and killing the futures of their children. Finally technology provided a communication source that no one can control, and these revolutions are the manifestations of that. For once the truth is winning there.

With the revolutions in Egypt, Libya, and Syria, there is a chance that when they get true democracy, they will elect Islamic Radicals to represent them. This would be a complete disaster and it would prove all the doubters, regarding the Arab Awakening, right. Many said that democracy is not the immediate answer to their concerns because they would elect terrorists to represent them. A similar situation happened in the Gaza Strip (Palestinian territory). When they finally got democracy they elected Hamas, a terrorist group, to represent them. This is their last chance, innovation and democracy doesn't come easy anywhere especially in the Middle East. I hope these fledgling democracies are very careful and choose wisely, instead of electing people who want to destroy Israel, who despise the United States, and do not want peace but, rather, a constant state of war. 21st century progressive leadership needs to be elected to transform the Arab countries into strong democracies. This would give children and adults every opportunity possible to live happy, productive, safe, and meaningful lives. The fact that Israel is the cause of all of the Arabs' problems is just a myth.

Most leaders in the Arab world only care about staying in power by any means necessary, they do not care about the Arab street. If Israel did not exist and the Palestinians owned and controlled all the land that is now Israel, the rest of the Arab and Iranian world would still have every single problem that they do now, probably worse, because there would be a king or dictator in that fictitious (for the purpose of this hypothetical) Palestinian state. And that theoretical Palestinian dictator would be supporting Assad and all the other ruthless dictators. The great lie is that every negative thing in the Arab world and the Persian world is Israel's or America's fault. The current leadership in the Middle East has been using this calamitous lie over and over, and it is designed to make Arabs and Persians ignore the real problems of their countries and continue to support terrible leaders. If I was a dictator, and I was robbing my people of everything and slaughtering them, would I tell them the truth? No, because they would oust me from power. I would make up something that they could all rally around, the Israel lie, and take attention away from the real source of their problems. Those leaders treat their populations like ignorant dogs and their populations get excited and play right into their hands. Egypt, for example, has a country and an economy to build why are they so concerned about Israel (a country they have a peace treaty with)?

In this life you do not get many chances to change everything for yourself and the future of your people-move forward and choose the right path. I know there are good moderate intellectual people in the Arab world: doctors, lawyers, teachers, and engineers, etc. who want to see honest leadership, hope for real lives, strong economies, educational opportunities, jobs, chances for raising a real family, children not being sacrificed for terrorism (either on the receiving or the giving end) and the chance to finally live without fear of their own government. Now is your time, you must seize this opportunity, believe me when I tell you it is the last one you have. Don't let the animals take control-we have all seen what happens in the Islamic world or any other world when extremists are in control and it is not good for anyone.

My vision is that democracy will spread throughout the Middle East and that movement will create secular democracies in Arab countries. That is the solution to the Middle East crisis. I am not naive and I know how democracy has utterly failed so far in Gaza and Lebanon. They have democratically elected Islamic Radicals to lead them and that is terrible and a complete waste of an opportunity for peace. The Arab Awakening is very different. Unlike those places there seem to be well-educated moderate people in the Arab countries who want democracy. This can be their chance to take over leadership and change everything. For any of the Middle East countries that are becoming democracies, the choice is easy. In a purely scientific analysis without religion, hate for Israel, and the rest of the artificial negative man made barriers to peace, ask yourself, who has the better quality of life, people in Gaza, Lebanon, and Iran (Islamic Radicals) or Americans and Europeans (secular democracies)? If freedom of speech, human rights, money, a free press, opportunity, and most importantly a peaceful long life for your children are important, the choice is clear.

If you want to live in a country where Islamic Radicals are in charge, move to Iran you have that option. Be strong and fight for your country-there is nothing more important in this world and in this life, other than faith for the religious, than that for you. You can go down in history as the generation that miraculously changed everything in the world, or you can be a footnote of a short lived hope followed by a war. Don't we already have enough of those types of footnotes? And if you can't let the Palestinian thing go-do you think you would have a bigger impact on helping the Palestinians if you were a real democracy run by moderates or a government run by a radical Islamic group or another dictator? How much has Assad or Iran done for the Palestinians? The proof is out there. Jordan, moderates, has had a much bigger role in the Palestinian peace process than Iran or Syria. Does the U.S. or Europe ever invite people like Assad or Ahmadinejad when they have multilateral peace talks about the Palestinian issue? No they do not, so the course some of you are following-in the name of the Palestinians supposedly-is to permanently not have a seat at the peace table. It is a losing approach with a 0% success rate. If the Middle East really wants to be democratic and progressive they should get the support of the entire world. What people want in the Arab world is very easy. The swift removal of completely corrupt, tyrannical, and barbaric leadership, the chance to raise and educate a family that has hope of a future in a secure environment, more rights for women (meaning that is what the women want) and democracy. They also want what makes democracies work: freedom of speech, freedom of assembly, and freedom of the press. Are these things we cannot help our supposed enemies get if it will no longer make them our enemies? My view on what they want is an interpretation based on what people on the ground from Egypt, Yemen, Libya, and Syria have said, done, and shared.

The U.S. doesn't have to be an invasion force where we lose lots of lives and replace governments with incompetent leaders. We can be more of a rescue force and save lives by helping people's home made revolutions. We can be a new 21st century version of what France did for us in the American Revolution. The U.S. saved thousands of lives in Libya by slowly forming a coalition with France and the U.K. That can be done in places such as Syria. It doesn't have to be all or nothing. We can use much less economic and military resources than we are currently using in our wars, to get a much higher return on a wider scale by getting involved in much smaller, in both scope and time commitment, missions. If we got out of Afghanistan, as was explained in the "Afghanistan" chapter, we could use a fraction of the price of that war to take care of all military business if every single penny was accounted for and things were done right. What people do not understand about Afghanistan is that if the entire Middle East is democratic (however long that takes), Afghanistan will take care of itself. We need to get out of Afghanistan, while providing air support there whenever their government wants it. We cannot abandon them completely and we do not need to.

We have been in Iraq for over eight years and the American death toll is about 4600. We have been in Afghanistan for eleven years and the death toll is 1600. The people were not calling for us, but we went to theoretically fight for democracy, to free them. In Syria, 80,000 people, including many children, have been massacred in two years. Precisely because they want democracy and they are exercising freedom of speech. Syria's dictator has more ties to terrorism, Hezbollah, and Iran than Sadam Hussein ever did. The world needs to do something substantial to stop the wholesale massacre and get rid of Assad. How many Syrian lives will it take, 100 thousand, 200, 300? If Arabs around the Middle East really care about their Muslim brothers and sisters, they should help them in Syria when no one else will. Give them military support. Jordan, Egypt, and Saudi Arabia are more than capable to help if they work together. We all know Assad is on life support and he has a year or two more max until he is ousted, do more innocents really have to die waiting for the inevitable? It is so tragic and heart breaking that these civilians are dying especially in light of the fact that they are so close to getting what they want. Many won't be able to enjoy the fruits of their courage and bravery and they are so close, it's devastating really. Whether the world helps or not, the people in Syria will win there and the next government will be free of Assad. The question is how offensive does the world want to be to that next government, meaning how many children, women, and men have to be sacrificed for them to win without help? If the world helped I'm sure the new Syrian government would reward that with real friendship. We can save children's lives. Why is it always should we invade or not? That is so pedestrian. There are many more effective and efficient ways to do things now than sending and risking the lives of human beings, who are our citizens, on a mass level, invasion style. It is called air support and special ops. That is as low risk and high return as you can get in the theatre of war.

The leader of the opposition in Syria says when they get rid of Assad he would cut relations with Iran and Hezbollah. That is the answer to the troubles of the Middle East: democracies whose main concern is their own people and extending economic and humanitarian measures so their people can live normal lives. Stop with supplying terrorists and the fighting. The game is no longer about war, it is about money, human rights, and the exchange of information and tools to make life better for everyone everywhere. For example, Israel has cutting edge technology on how to provide water for the Middle East whose countries are currently facing a water crisis. Once the Arab countries and Iran have democracies, the next step is peace treaties with Israel and then a peace treaty with the Palestinians. Then Israel can share its technologies with the region for peace. With all the natural resources this region has and the hunger and passion of its people, the sky is the limit. I truly believe that with some bold leadership, that could help all sides with the process, and the right people this can get done in 20 years maximum. A bright future where every man in the Middle East, whether he is Jewish, Muslim, or Christian, can live as neighbors and brothers working for the great things life has to offer: family, profession, science, technology, music, the arts, travel, education, and religious beliefs, not fighting and war. Like it or not that is the future, a future where people do not have to leave their native homes, which they love, to provide a normal life of peace and opportunity for their family. My family had to do that and so did many other people I know. This is all going to happen. All we have to do is believe.

Conclusion

When people are insecure and have no confidence in themselves it is easy to constantly question their actions and engage in negative thoughts. That is why much of the American public constantly wonders and second guesses every single thing the government does and expects failure. For example, much of the American public no longer gives the government the benefit of the doubt, they give the government the detriment of the doubt. Sometimes this is justified, but many other times it is not. We live in dangerous times and the American public, many times, does not understand the complexity of the context in which governmental actions are taken. They repeat what they hear in the media.

The most important function of the American President is making sure American people do not get taken hostage, murdered, or tortured. Life is our most precious gift and must be protected against assassins and human animals in whatever form they take. I believe that the United States is ready to spread this right along with other basic rights across the world. Currently, how many human rights a human being has is a direct consequence of what geographic location is their arbitrary birthplace. For example, if a woman is born in the U.S. she has many human rights and if she is born in Saudi Arabia she has none.

It is our moral responsibility to spread human rights, freedom of religion, and equal rights for women and men across the world. We are all in this world together and we must fight for progress. We must stop being childish and start having a more intellectually sophisticated view of our place in the world. We must stop thinking that we are just a country and our country is all that matters. Think of the world. Imagine how much farther we could progress as a people if the entire world was democratic and on the same page. We finally have the resources to try to do that, and most people would rather just bail out and hide in the United States rather than go out and grab life and the world by the horns. If the entire world had a political system that was democratic and inspired, the de facto system that cultivates the best minds in politics, the arts, and science, we would truly have a beautiful world. We could make the type of progress in fifty years that would take two hundred in the current system. God did not intend the type of world we live in. Join me in my quest to make this happen. I do not just believe, I know we can make do it. I realize that normally it takes time for humanity to catch up to visionaries. Whether it is now or in a hundred or two hundred years, my vision of the world will come to fruition, or the human race will destroy the world. Those are the only two viable options. We will either completely come together or completely come apart.

By reading this book and supporting me, I am giving you the opportunity to join to fight for what we should all hold most dear. That is human rights, freedom of religion, and equality for all races, members of all religions, and women. Not just in the United States, as simple-minded people would think, but in the entire world. Imagine a theoretical United States of the World. Philosophically you cannot reconcile that you support basic rights and freedoms for yourself, but not for others. If you have freedom and someone else does not, no matter where he is geographically, you must fight to provide freedom. How can you possibly justify a person having no human rights or religious freedom, just because of where he happened to be born geographically? In Iran, recently, a man was flogged 84 times because he had premarital sex and because he got drunk. In Pakistan a teacher who told his students that Mohammad did not become a Muslim until his forties, which is true, was executed. Trust me that is not what God wants. Just because you do not know about atrocities or because they are not happening in your country does not mean they are not happening. The time has come to free the world.

Our generation and the younger ones are so much more versatile and fluent with the greatest, most powerful, and peaceful invention that mankind has ever had: the internet. However, other old people who are not as fluent or knowledgeable at all with this all-encompassing invention are the ones in charge of making decisions on our behalf. It is not right and makes no sense. They are living in the wrong lost artificial world that time and technology has passed by, not us. Television media is even a dinosaur now. It is hard to come to grips with this, but the reality is that the internet is more powerful than the television or our government. That is why everything seems so messed up, because governmental power is in the hands of the wrong people. We need to grasp the power to start making decisions that are the right ones for our generation, the younger ones, and, quite frankly, the world. The reason it will take some time is because it must be done peacefully. That has to be the way. In history most movements that have everything on their side have to do it by war and sacrificing lives. We cannot and must not to do that. We can be the best history has ever seen, and that is what we will be.

Make no mistake, this will be a revolution of sorts. It is a communication and informational revolution of ideas and the sharing of those ideas with the world in the quickest format (internet), and it is completely peaceful. If we can finish it well, however long it takes, it is the answer and the solution. We can take on anything and win. At this point it's all about details and patience. We have been given this great amazing gift of the internet and its true importance is that people from all over the world, regardless of religion, race, or whatever else can now communicate at lightning speed. Let's use it to fix everything. The real world just needs some time to catch up, and that is only natural and fine. Be a little patient.

I truly hope, dream, and believe that everything can work out. In the history of the world there has never been a way to communicate like this. It is a cliche but real communication is the key to everything, talking not fighting.

We can do this. Just imagine if someday our generation, and the younger ones, can figure out world peace. That is making history. I am not saying the odds are on our side. I'm a realist. Together we can make anything happen, that is the truth. With the right mindset and everyone on the same page, our government, and every single democratic government in the world working together, have the capacity to do great things. We can feed the hungry in Africa, we can eradicate AIDS and other disease, we can bring peace and freedom to the Middle East and Africa, and we can give human rights, freedom of religion, and democracy to the entire world. It is our moral imperative.

The difference between me and leaders in the U.S., or rather politicians, as they don't seem to qualify as "leaders", is that I never wasted time meeting political "bigwigs" or going to fundraisers and playing the political game. I've been paying close attention to every Presidential election since 1984, when I was ten years old, and I've read books about real historical leaders from all over the world since I was a child. I know how they did it, and what worked and what did not. Instead of taking care of business and solving problems, American politicians' priorities are following polls and seeing what the media says everyday and responding to that, either indirectly or directly. That is not leadership it is nonsense. Citizens elect politicians to do the job and then the campaign is over, so try doing the job and then when running for re-election, they can vote for an individual based on his/

her record, rather than how many times a candidate opens his mouth. People elect politicians because they think those running for office can do a better job than them, so at least try that.

By writing this book, what I want to do is start a third political party for every rational American who wants to move forward. I do not want to involve myself in the constant animosity between the two traditional parties in the United States. They are so busy attacking each other, almost constantly, that they simply do not have their minds on problem solving and solutions oriented policy. It is not just politicians, the media has taken sides and it seems like everyday when watching the news channels on television or listening to the radio, instead of discussing issues like adults, both sides attack each other like children. It is simply not possible, in this atmosphere, to work optimally as a government or a people. I want my party to attract politicians that are concerned about doing things instead of bickering all the time. The country is sick of the status quo and so am I quite frankly. The United States has two options: continue in the current format, see where it leads, or join me, try something new, and let's apply real, well thought out solution oriented ideas to tackle the world's problems.